The English Language in Medieval Literature

The English Language in Medieval Literature

NORMAN BLAKE

Professor of English Language
University of Sheffield

Methuen
London and New York

First published in 1977
by J. M. Dent & Sons Ltd
Aldine House, 33 Welbeck Street, London W1M 8LX

First published as a University Paperback in 1979
by Methuen & Co. Ltd
11 New Fetter Lane, London EC4P 4EE

Published in the USA
by Methuen & Co.
an associate company of Methuen, Inc.
733 Third Avenue, New York, NY 10017

© *1979 N. F. Blake*

Printed in Great Britain at the
University Press, Cambridge

ISBN 0 416 72470 1

British Library Cataloguing in Publication Data

Blake, Norman Francis
  The English language in medieval literature.
  – (University paperbacks; 670).
  1. English literature – Middle English,
  1100–1500 – History and criticism 2. English
  language – Middle English, 1100–1500 – Style
  I. Title II. Series
  820'.9'001   PR255
  ISBN 0-416-72470-1

Contents

Preface

This book is an attempt to show how a knowledge of the English language of the medieval period helps us to understand the nature and type of literature written then. It builds upon the work done by philologists and literary critics; it does not attempt to replace that work. One of the problems in reading the literature of an earlier period is that we find it difficult to shed our current linguistic attitudes although the English of an earlier period is very different in structure from our own. This is as much a problem in reading Shakespeare as it is in reading medieval literature, though the adjustments we need to make to our awareness of language is different in each case. It is of course possible to read medieval literature or Shakespeare as though it is modern literature, but as C. S. Lewis suggested in *An Experiment in Criticism* for any deep reading of a literary work it is better to understand what conditions produced it. One of the most important of these conditions is the language in which it was written. Therefore I have taken as a starting point the typical attitudes a modern reader brings to any work of literature because of his acquaintance with modern English in both its spoken and written forms.

I have assumed it necessary first to show how we may misread earlier literature because of our unconscious linguistic assumptions. This has meant showing what is not possible in medieval English literature because of the state of the language at that time, and I have considered in depth examples chosen from Old and Middle English. It might seem after a cursory reading that I have concentrated too much on what is not, rather than what is, possible. But in each of the examples discussed I try to show both the strengths and the weaknesses of medieval English literature. Unfortunately the subtleties of medieval literature are not those of modern literature, and there is always the danger that some readers find it difficult to accept as subtleties those literary artifices which are not used in modern literature. The purpose of the book then is preparatory.

It shows some of the adjustments we should make in order to read medieval literature with profit; but it does not seek to supply a grand theory of medieval literature, though naturally the various chapters are informed by a unified view of the subject. The way I have organized the book has led to the restatement of certain basic theories. After the first two chapters which are of a general nature, the other chapters are devoted to more specialized topics. In writing the book this way I intended that individual chapters should stand independently so that they could be used in seminars and be discussed in the light of the texts students were reading at that time. Such discussions may naturally lead to the modification of my views or to the establishment of more literary theories on the basis of those views.

The approach outlined in this book is appropriate at this time for several reasons. The two principal methods of investigating medieval literature, source study and philology, have come under increasing attack. While source study remains an important part of literary investigation, many feel it has been studied too exclusively as an end in itself, whereas the origins of a particular theme or narrative are of interest only if they help to explain the text in English. A fuller understanding of the linguistic environment may help us to appreciate how a foreign theme is transmuted into a piece of English literature. Philology which placed great store on the examination of cruces, dialect peculiarities and linguistic minutiae in texts has been abandoned by many. The new fashion of reading literature 'as literature' has had its impact on the medieval period so that many critical theories have been imported from later periods of English and applied indiscriminately to the medieval period. Few have bothered to consider how suitable such theories are in the early period, though this may have been for lack of time because critical fashions have come and gone so rapidly. The result is that many students read medieval literature without having any feel for or understanding of the language in which the works were written. Teachers often deplore this lack of a language basis in modern teaching and scholarship, but as philology is considered so outmoded they have not known how to satisfy this felt need.

The method outlined in this book may go a little way to meet that deficiency, for it is the basis of this book that an understanding of the language and its limitations is fundamental in any evaluation of the literature of the period. Advances in language work in this century are usually associated with modern linguistics, though the help that this new study can give students of medieval literature has not been evaluated so far. I have not attempted to write a critique of medieval literature using linguistic terminology, for that

8

would be a meaningless exercise. For the most part I have avoided using linguistic terminology. Nevertheless, I have tried to keep constantly in mind the advances made by linguistics in our understanding of the way language works: I have attempted to apply some of those advances to the study of the medieval period. One of the basic insights of modern linguistics is that language should be studied synchronically as well as diachronically, that is that the study of individual periods in a language is as important as the study of its historical development. The former has been too neglected as far as the medieval period is concerned and a new approach to its literature based on the synchronic study of language is long overdue. I may add, however, that I feel my book is only a beginning in the attempt to use the insights of modern linguistics in our appreciation of medieval literature.

The germ of this book is my inaugural lecture at Sheffield delivered early in 1974 and subsequently printed in a modified form in *Studia Neophilologica* 48, 1976. I gratefully acknowledge the permission of the editors of that journal to re-use some of the material from my lecture again. The lecture was also read to several medieval societies in other universities and I am indebted to the many comments made by my various audiences. I should like to thank my colleagues in the Department of English Language at Sheffield for many fruitful discussions on language and medieval literature over the years. One of my research students, Mrs Lilian McCobb, deserves a special word of thanks for suggesting several lines of enquiry to me. Donald Matthew kindly read through my typescript and made many suggestions as to how it might be improved. I would also like to thank my secretary, Mrs Janice Campbell, for preparing the typescript.

I

The Literary Background

INTRODUCTORY
The interaction of language and literature is frequently propounded, if rarely analysed. In this book I seek to explain how the state of the English language in the medieval period (from the earliest Old English records to about 1500) influenced the sort of literature that was composed and the manner in which it was written. To understand that interaction it is essential to have some appreciation of the differences in language and literature then and now, for one of the most difficult imaginative leaps a reader faces in approaching the literature of any past age is the abandoning of those attitudes subconsciously assimilated simply by reading and talking contemporary English. Although we know Chaucer's English is old, we nevertheless think of it as English and so feel that we can understand it without much difficulty. As a result we make insufficient allowance for the way his language differs from ours. Paradoxically it may be less deceptive for an Englishman to read a foreign literature, say Greek, or for a foreigner to read Chaucer precisely because in these cases we do make allowance for the cultural gap between us and what we are reading and so consciously seek to bridge the distance that separates us from the time in which the author lived. We are more conscious of the linguistic differences and so attempt to make the necessary compensation.

It is therefore necessary to stress the different attitudes that existed then, and this can only be done by comparing them with our own present-day ones. If, for example, we take the idea of literature itself we can see how it has changed over the years. The word *literature* originally meant 'a letter, what is written'; and this is not a bad definition for the medieval period in that all written documents other than household accounts and such like were considered to be literature. The later association of literature with *belles lettres* and more recently with works of outstanding emotional and aesthetic appeal has led to a narrowing of the term.[1] Today we do not expect a novelist to write sermons, and few would include modern sermons in their definition of what constitutes literature. Even a novel has to be of a certain approved standard to qualify as literature; hack work is dismissed as unworthy of serious consideration and therefore by implication as not being literature. This has led both to an increasing specialization among authors who may not be familiar with the vocabulary of works which fall outside literature, and to the reader adopting certain expectations in respect of the works he will read. The vocabulary of different types of work will vary and we are easily thrown off balance when writers do not observe the proprieties of composition. A different set of expectations existed in the Middle Ages. Chaucer could turn his hand to a sermon, a bawdy tale, a philosophical or technical treatise, and a romance. Medieval authors moved from one level of literary production to another without apparent difficulty. This meant that they employed a much less specialized vocabulary than we are used to now. Words of a religious meaning had a much wider and commoner usage than we now give to them, and we may misinterpret medieval works if we force their vocabulary into restricted fields of meaning by a too rigorous application of the genre convention.

In this book I shall also take literally the definition of *literature* as 'what is written'; I shall concern myself with the written records that remain rather than with the possibility that many of the poems existed orally before being committed to writing. The arguments for and against a flourishing oral literature before the development of written literature are involved and need not concern us here. The literary works that survive have come down to us in a written form and it seems most sensible to confine our attention to that form. This point needs emphasizing because it has been claimed that the particular stylistic traits of medieval literature are the result of the oral background of that literature.[2] However, I will suggest that most of these features can be adequately explained by the linguistic and literary constraints operative at the time without recourse to this assumed oral background. I hasten to add that such an explanation does not in itself disprove the notion of an earlier oral stage, for before the invention of tape recorders there was no way of preserving oral literature in an oral form. For literary purposes the existence of an earlier oral literature can be ignored as we have no way of knowing what it was like. There is no evidence to prove that the characteristics of oral literature today would also be found in the oral literature of the past when conditions and expectations were so different.

It is also necessary to emphasize that this book is about the linguistic conditions and literature of medieval England. Although what I write about England may have some relevance to other European countries, conditions in each were quite diverse. What is true of one medieval literature does not automatically apply to another. Because we live in a fragmented world today, there is a temptation to look back at the Middle Ages as a time when men's outlook and behaviour followed uniform patterns throughout Western Europe, for the presence of Latin and the Catholic Church provided unifying forces. Similarly because the alliterative line is acknowledged to be a Germanic form and because various heroic stories were current in both England and Scandinavia, we all too easily assume that all stories were widely known and that what is absent in one literature may be supplied from another. A moment's reflection will expose the improbability of this view. The Middle Ages extended over a long period and Western Europe covers an extensive area. Conditions were never uniform, and although there were many universal influences at work they affected different areas and times in different ways.

By the same token although I am dealing with a period in English literature extending over more than eight hundred years, I would not wish the reader to think that conditions were uniform throughout this time. The language of Chaucer is not the language of *Beowulf*, and literary conditions at the end of the Middle Ages were very different from those which were operative at the beginning of our period. Nevertheless, in comparison with the modern literary and linguistic environment there are enough points of similarity in the English Middle Ages to warrant taking the period as a whole. My aim is not to suggest a massive and deadening uniformity for eight hundred years of literary activity; it is more modest. It is simply to show a modern reader what adjustments he must make in his own attitudes in order to appreciate medieval English literature more fruitfully. At the rather general level of this book, those adjustments will be virtually the same for reading Chaucer as for reading *Beowulf*.

EXTENT AND SURVIVAL OF ENGLISH LITERATURE

A feature of the medieval period is that there were, comparatively speaking, very few works in English. This does not mean that there was a lack of literary activity or even indeed that there has been a wholesale destruction of manuscripts. The example of Bede (673–735) shows that from the beginning of the medieval period written works were produced in considerable numbers. Such works were usually in Latin, which was felt to be the most suitable medium of communication. It could be claimed that at first writing and Latin were synonymous. Latin was an international language and Bede's audience would have been smaller if he had written in Old English. Latin was also a relatively static language, being a dead language, and it was not subject to dialectal variations. There may be different dialect versions of the Old English *Cædmon's Hymn* (c. 670), but Bede's Latin paraphrase of it in his *Historia ecclesiastica* (731) is uniform in all manuscripts of that work, whether they were written in Northumbria or Wessex or even indeed abroad. As there was at first little tradition of writing in Old English, educated men naturally chose Latin as the language to use in written works. Ironically it may have been the Danish invasions in the ninth century which inspired the production of works in Old English. We know that King Alfred made or had made translations of several Latin prose works. Scholars now accept that much Old English poetry was Christian and moral, which suggests the poems were produced as part of an educational programme. So it may be that many of the scriptural poems at least were written to educate people in much the same way as Alfred's translations. Furthermore, the use made by Ælfric of Old English poetry in the late tenth century suggests that the alliterative poetic form still retained for him its vigour and appeal. Yet although Old English is far richer than most other contemporary vernacular literatures, it is abjectly poor in comparison with the output of Latin literature. Even if we could date most Old English poetry to the latter three centuries of the Old English period, it would still mean that about 30,000 lines have to be distributed over 250 years; the amount is insufficient to talk seriously of any tradition.

The position is much the same in the Middle English period, but for somewhat different reasons. With the Norman Conquest there was an influx of French speakers into England. For many years French was the first language of a large number of Englishmen, and Anglo-Norman, its English form, was a living language. Many works were written in French, usually in the Anglo-Norman variety, in England and some famous French texts would have been lost if they had not survived in copies made in England. At the same time Latin continued to flourish and the output of works in that language was not lessened. Richard Rolle (c. 1300–49), for example, found it natural to write in Latin and he used English only for those works addressed to his female disciples who were ignorant of Latin. It was not simply religious works which were written in Latin. The Arthur story made its first major appearance in Geoffrey of Monmouth's *Historia regum Britanniæ* (c. 1137), and legal and other technical documents continued to appear in that language. Although English was used by some writers, its use was sporadic and usually for a particular purpose, as in the case of Rolle. The result is that texts often seem to appear quite fortuitously without past or future; they are not part of a native vernacular tradition. There is nothing in the twelfth century to prepare us for the appearance of *The Owl and the Nightingale* from the early thirteenth century and it gave rise to no imitations or developments later in that century; it stands in splendid isolation. It was only in the fourteenth and fifteenth centuries that there was a pronounced upsurge in the production of works in English. French ceased to be used as a spoken language in England: Parliament and the courts now conducted their business in English, and schools used it as their medium of instruction. The Hundred Years' War may have inspired a feeling of nationalism among the English with a consequent increase in the use of the English language, though Latin of course was still an important force both at a spoken level and in literature. English became accepted as the language of speech, but it had yet to win recognition as the best medium of written works. French and Latin were still regarded as the best languages for literary expression so that the fourteenth and fifteenth centuries witnessed a great vogue in translation. In this way Englishmen hoped to transfer some of the prestige of the original language to the English translation. These languages were still the norm which English imitated. Though writing in English grew tremendously in the fourteenth and fifteenth centuries, the reasons behind this growth were not very different from those which produced the vernacular works of the ninth and tenth centuries. But whereas the Norman Conquest had stifled that particular growth of English through the introduction of Anglo-Norman, at the end of the Middle Ages English was allowed to develop without restraint. It was the writers of the Elizabethan Age who were the primary beneficiaries of that development. If there had been no Norman Conquest it is possible that a vernacular literature as rich as that of the Elizabethan period might have developed in the twelfth or thirteenth century.

If works in English were produced more sporadically, their survival was also more uncertain for they were copied less frequently. English works were produced most often for instructional purposes and sufficient copies were made to satisfy that demand. Usually that meant a limited number of copies for local use, though some religious texts had a wider appeal throughout the country. Naturally works in English were read only in England, another factor which restricted the number of copies made. If an English work was considered sufficiently important, like Rolle's *The Form of Living* (1348-9), it would be translated into Latin so that it could reach a bigger audience. In the Old English period it is normal to find that English poems survive in one manuscript. The notable exception is *Cædmon's Hymn* which is extant in seventeen manuscripts. This poem is exceptional because the Old English version was written in the margin of many Latin manuscripts of Bede's *Historia ecclesiastica,* which are numerous, and because an English translation of Bede's work was made which had the poem inserted at the appropriate place. The poem survives in so many copies simply because it had a close link with a Latin text, not because people wanted to preserve this particular Old English poem. Works in Latin were produced in multiple copies because monastic scriptoria were the only places where manuscripts were written. The monasteries were concerned to preserve works of the fathers like Bede which were read and studied throughout Western Europe; the copying of English poems was carried out only when particular reasons demanded it. It is true that some Old English prose works like the *Anglo-Saxon Chronicle* and the religious writings of Ælfric (955–*c.* 1012) survive in many copies, but this is because they were associated with the educational reforms of Alfred and of the tenth-century Benedictine revival. English was given priority at times like these because Latin was insufficiently familiar to Englishmen.

In the early Middle English period the situation is much the same. A text like Laȝamon's *Brut* (*c.* 1200) is extant in two copies, although at least one other manuscript is known to have existed. The French text on which the *Brut* is based, Wace's poem of the same name, survives in about thirty manuscripts. Wace used as his source Geoffrey of Monmouth's *Historia regum Britanniæ* of which almost two hundred manuscripts are known, and about fifty of them are from the twelfth century. Clearly it is much more likely that a later writer would have known and been influenced by Geoffrey's Latin work or even Wace's French version than by Laȝamon's poem. This is an important consideration which needs constantly to be borne in mind, for most modern readers' ignorance of Latin and their study only of English medieval literature combine to undervalue this fact. The exception to this general rule of the small number of copies of English works is formed again by those texts which were produced for a more educational or religious purpose. Works like the *Ancrene Wisse* (*c.* 1225) and Rolle's English treatises are extant in many copies because they were used as teaching manuals and so treasured by monastic and other religious institutions. Their influence was, however, limited because of their particular reading public. Right at the end of the medieval period the position regarding secular texts changed because it then became common to issue some English works in multiple copies. At this period secular bookshops came into being which were specifically set up to produce literary works for sale to merchants and aristocrats. *The Canterbury Tales* and *Confessio Amantis* from the end of the fourteenth century exist in numerous luxury manuscripts and both works were printed by Caxton. It would be as surprising to discover a sixteenth-century gentleman who was ignorant of the existence of *The Canterbury Tales* as it would be to discover a thirteenth-century one who was aware of the existence of Laȝamon's *Brut*. However, at this period the multiplication of literary texts in English was confined to those produced in the south in the area around London. *Sir Gawain and the Green Knight* and many other poems in the alliterative tradition are extant in single copies.

AUTHOR AND AUDIENCE
Many works of the medieval English period are anonymous, though the majority of those authors whose names are known were clerics of one sort or another. This is certainly the case in Old English where Cynewulf in the ninth century was a monk and Cædmon in the eighth was associated with the monastery at Whitby. The prose writers, particularly those from the late tenth century like Ælfric and Wulfstan, were invariably in orders. The only exception is King Alfred who was responsible for initiating the educational revival of the late ninth century and who himself made some of the translations which form part of that revival. But the helpers he recruited were mostly monks; he was himself assisted by Bishop Asser, and the main emphasis of his activity was on revitalizing the religious life of the country as the books translated indicate. The Middle English period shows little change, particularly at first. Though we know little of Laȝamon, the author of the *Brut*, or Nicholas of Guildford, the presumed author of *The Owl and the Nightingale*, both were priests. The *Ancrene Wisse* was written by a spiritual guide who would have been a priest, as indeed were the other writers in the contemplative tradition. The contribution of the Franciscans to the production of Middle English lyrics is now better understood, and probably clerics drafted the plays of the Corpus Christi cycles. It is agreed that William Langland was at least in minor orders, and many of the translations from the fourteenth and fifteenth centuries were made by chaplains to the nobility like John Trevisa. Even in the fifteenth century monkish authors were common enough as the cases of John Lydgate and Osbern Bokenham show. A change does begin to manifest itself in the fourteenth century. At the beginning of that century the bookshops that had been established in and around London were run as commercial enterprises, and they may have been staffed by professional scribes rather than by clerics. The staple output of such shops was translation, for they sought to provide English copies of fashionable French reading matter. Another indication of the change in authorship is seen in the careers of Chaucer and Gower, both of whom were members of the middle

classes. The son of a vintner, Chaucer became a civil servant. Gower, who may have been from the lesser gentry, was a lawyer. Each had his own career, and writing was a leisure pursuit rather than a full-time occupation supported by a religious institution. These two are in some ways exceptional even in the fourteenth century, though they show how things were developing.

The importance of the clerical and anonymous nature of medieval English literature cannot be over emphasized. The situation in France provides a suitable contrast. In France there were many centres of literary production which were usually the courts of local magnates. Characteristic of that country is the small court where the local count or countess would patronize literary works and so attract the services of professional authors or of noblemen with literary pretensions. Such authors were proud of their work and they were respected for it. The works were known to be by particular individuals and literature developed a more personal note. We know the names and careers of many more French than English authors. The atmosphere at some of these courts was no doubt highly charged, for they were the breeding grounds of new poetic talents which would be immediately recognized and acclaimed. Poets often referred to each other's works and seem to have been writing within a tight, closely-knit tradition.[3]

Things were different in England. In the Middle English period the absence of local patronage of English secular literature is attributable to the Norman Conquest which left England with a French-speaking aristocracy which looked to France for its cultural inspiration. English had to emerge as a language of possible courtly composition before its writings could be actively encouraged in noble households under the patronage of local aristocrats. It may be significant that the best known aristocratic writer in England in the medieval period is a Frenchman, Charles of Orleans. He spent many years as a captive in England waiting for his ransom to be paid; he used his enforced leisure to introduce the concept of writing as an aristo-cratic pursuit. The result was that some fifteenth-century English gentlemen followed his example, though the full flowering of court literature took place only in the sixteenth century. In the Old English period the absence of a tightly-knit literary community was caused by the predominant position of the Church and by the failure to develop the ideal that courts should act as the focus for secular literary pursuits. While the recitation of poetry at the king's hall was a literary theme, this theme does not reflect what actually happened, for most poetry was composed within a monastic environ-ment. Even Alfred devoted himself to encouraging composition in the monasteries. There is no Alfredian court poetry.

Within a local court a close-knit audience will develop who will appreciate local references and echoes from the works of known poets. The religious author, on the other hand, may be working within an established tradition of writing, but will often have a wider audience in mind than his immediate recipients. That the audience of medieval English literature was disparate and dispersed is insufficiently appreciated, for modern scholarship frequently assumes that poets in particular were writing for a restricted and homogeneous audience. Thus the digressions in *Beowulf* which deal with various Germanic heroes are considered to be so familiar that members of the audience would know the details intimately and hence understand what the poet was hinting at. The poet would have to know his audience well to take this risk. In most cases he tells us as much as is necessary for an appreciation of his main story. Whether all members of his audience knew the stories behind the allusions cannot be proved; it certainly seems unlikely that the audience was as well informed as we like to think. The same applies to the Old English poem *Deor* which is built on a series of examples of unfortunate people. There were stories behind these brief references, but one does not have to know them to appreciate the poem. The situation is perhaps paralleled by what happens in my own classes. If I say to my students that Beowulf was as strong as Samson, they accept the validity of the comparison even though few, if any, can tell me the biblical story of Samson. Samson is the prototype of a strong man, though ideas about him are often hazy. Similarly in Middle English it is improbable that the audience was as close-knit as is often implied by modern scholarship. For example, it is claimed that Chaucer introduced a reference to the lyric 'My lief is faren in londe' in *The Nun's Priest's Tale*. Many assume that its occurrence here proves that it was widely known by the 1390s even though it survives only in a manuscript from about 1500[4]. This need not be the correct inference. Chaucer was for his time a widely read man who introduced into his poetry references from many foreign writers who can hardly have been known even by name to many of his contemporaries. If the evidence of manuscript corruption is any guide, the scribes who copied his poems were ignorant of many of the personal and place names included by Chaucer from his wide reading. If we can accept that he introduced esoteric references to foreign authors or learned concepts, why do we have to assume that any English poem or person referred to was well known? Why must we assume that he behaved differently in each case? While it may be true that lyrics like 'My lief is faren in londe' were well known, there is no need to accept they were, and we cannot use the assumed reference to it in Chaucer as any proof

that it was. Each author draws from his own reading and knowledge, and these may not be typical of his time. The diffuseness
of the medieval audience would suggest that this rarely was the
case.

Even in such matters as metrical form it is difficult to detect the
presence of a homogeneous audience, for from copies made of medieval
poems it is clear that some scribes failed to understand the nature
of the verse they were copying. The most noteworthy examples are
those metres which have a short line such as a bob within the stanza.
One instance when the nature of this bob was completely misunderstood occurs in Wynkyn de Worde's print (*c.* 1530) of *The Quatrefoil
of Love*, a Northern poem written in the latter part of the fourteenth
century in the same metre as that used in the contemporaneous *Sir
Gawain and the Green Knight*. The bob was put on the right hand
side of the page in many manuscripts, and this was the position it
seems to have had in Wynkyn's copytext for when the compositor
set up the text he did not know what to do with it. The result is that
it was tacked on either to the line before or after, or the bob and
wheel were emended to make it into a better known type of metre.[5]
In Chaucer's *Sir Thopas* the bob is handled in different ways in the
various manuscripts. It would appear that there was no standard
way of writing out this type of stanza and so it is hardly surprising
that some copyists were not aware of the correct disposition of the
lines. In some manuscripts of *The Canterbury Tales* it is only in *Sir
Thopas* that the scribe introduced the bracketing of rhyme words.
While this feature occurs not infrequently in manuscripts of the
fourteenth and fifteenth centuries, its occurrence only in this poem
of *The Canterbury Tales* suggests that the scribes wanted to avoid
possible misunderstanding of the rhyme scheme which they thought
might occur. This attempt to avoid misunderstanding suggests they
were not sure of their audience. But the positioning of the bob-lines
and the use of bracketing in *Sir Thopas* is a complicated matter
which I shall not discuss further here.[6] I use the example simply to
underline the diffuseness of the audience, for if such a fundamental
feature as the metre of the poem was treated so differently by
various scribes what reason have we to suppose that the audience
was small and homogeneous? No doubt the difficulty of preserving
metrical forms was an important factor in restricting the use of
exotic metres: poems in the shape of butterflies or with words strung
across the page arise only with printing. The example in Stephen
Hawes's *The Conversion of Swearers* (1509) is probably the earliest of
its kind.

Two interrelated points have some bearing on the foregoing
remarks. The first is that seen from today the Middle Ages may

appear to be the heyday of forgery and plagiarism. The former is of greater importance in historical than in literary studies; the latter seems frequent in literature because authors drew extensively on the works of others, copying their themes and words quite blatantly. In a situation where literature is not considered a personal possession, plagiarism is hardly the right word for this type of borrowing. Texts were copied and adapted by anyone; they were treated as though they were public property. Once available they were part of the common good. It would be difficult for a reader or scribe to know whether what he was reading was the author's original or not – and this in its turn would lessen his interest in the author's original words. For example, in the fourteenth century *Piers Plowman* was revised twice by its author to give the three texts known today as the A, B and C versions. Some manuscripts of the A version contain an addition by John But, and other manuscripts of the poem contain a text which has been conflated from more than one version. How could a contemporary reader unravel these complexities when perhaps he had only one manuscript in front of him? In the previous century the *Ancrene Wisse* was adapted both by its author and by other writers for different audiences and purposes. A text was not regarded as an extension of its author's psychology in which his words are sacrosanct because they reveal, if only subconsciously, something of his make-up. Hence the biographical approach to medieval literature is unrewarding: we know a lot about Chaucer's life, but it provides us with little insight into his work.[7] The second point is that these conditions encouraged work that was general rather than individual, stereotyped rather than original. The vocabulary, themes and images became common property which were freely borrowed so that it is difficult, for example, to decide which anonymous poems were written by the same man. The authors used traditional expressions and clothed their thoughts in type characters and allegorical figures with little apparent individuality.

ABSENCE OF TRADITION

One most important result of all this is that there was no feeling of tradition in medieval English literature in the sense that people knew and remembered the words of English literary works. No single English text was sufficiently well known for an author to assume that his readers would be so familiar with it that he could allude to its verbal expressions. There was no one work which produced an echo as the Bible or Shakespeare does today. There was no sense of a past literary tradition which any author must take cognisance of lest he should otherwise be misunderstood for failing to realize the connotations of words which occur in familiar texts. Indicative of this lack of tradition is the fact that in general English writers refer only to the names of French, biblical or classical authors. In England stories may have been known, but they were not known in a particular version by a particular poet. The *Beowulf* poet mentions the stories of Finn and Sigurd; but we are not told to conjure up the version of these stories as recited in any given work, and we have no reason to believe that there were verbal echoes in these passages in *Beowulf* which would have led the contemporary audience to think of one particular version. Chaucer refers to French authors like Granson, to Italian authors like Petrarch, and to a whole host of biblical and classical authors. Apart from his reference to 'Moral Gower' in his epilogue to *Troilus and Criseyde,* he does not name any English author – and in this instance since he links Gower with Ralph Strode and calls him 'moral', he was clearly thinking of him not so much as a poet but as a moralist; no poem by Gower is mentioned. When he wants to refer to English works Chaucer simply mentions the names of heroes as in *Sir Thopas*:

> Men speken of romances of prys,
> Of Horn child and of Ypotys,
> Of Beves and sir Gy,
> Of sir Lybeux and Pleyndamour. (VII. 897–900)[8].

In this case as in many others not all the heroes are known to have been celebrated in English romances; there is no extant romance which deals with 'Pleyndamour'. It does not follow therefore that the reference in such cases was exclusively, or even necessarily, to English works. Chaucer may also have been familiar with contemporary alliterative poetry, for the Parson in the prologue to his tale refers to the style of 'rum, ram, ruf', and Chaucer himself imitates the alliterative style in occasional battle scenes, but he never mentions a particular alliterative poem or poet. An exception to this lack of reference to English poetry is his possible allusion to the lyric 'My lief is faren in londe' mentioned above, and it may not be without significance that this belongs to the genre which we consider the least individual in Middle English literature. To Chaucer English works were insufficiently authoritative or fashionable to be worth quoting or alluding to. Even Caxton in his advice to people to cultivate chivalry urges them to read the works of a French author, Jean Froissart. He holds up as models many English heroes, but none was glorified in a particular history or chronicle in English which he thinks it necessary to mention. Some of the editions of Chaucerian works issued by Caxton include a prologue, in which elaborate praise of the poet bulks large. Yet these prologues never include specific references to other works by Chaucer in order to develop a sense of the poet's œuvre. In the prologue to the second edition of *The Canterbury Tales* Caxton records that Chaucer 'made many bokes and treatyces of many a noble historye as wel in metre as in ryme and prose'⁹, but he does not name any of them. Even at this time it was unusual to think of a work as being by a particular man (Caxton issued *Troilus and Criseyde* without indicating it was by Chaucer) or to accept that a writer should be remembered by all his work. Only in one instance does Caxton mention the other works done by a writer. In his prologue to Trevisa's translation of Higden's *Polychronicon* he notes that Trevisa had also translated the Bible and the *De proprietatibus rerum* by Bartholomæus Anglicus. In this case his reason was to suggest that Trevisa was a worthy translator, whose work should therefore be acceptable to his clients; but in fact there is considerable doubt whether Trevisa actually did make a translation of the Bible.

The situation contrasts very sharply with Latin religious texts. In Latin texts the words of previous Latin authors are quoted and commented upon so that one gets the impression that each work is built on the foundation of the efforts of all previous writers on the subject. Texts form part of a whole; they do not stand in isolation. In English writings the words of an individual Latin author or text are frequently inserted. It is true that many of these quotations are traditional and some are inaccurate, but their inclusion does show that it was not ignorance of a framework of reference which led English authors to neglect quotations from other English texts. It was partly because English works were not considered authoritative and partly because they were not preserved in the original words of the author. This reasoning is confirmed by the only English quotations which are found in English texts, proverbial sayings. A poem like *The Owl and the Nightingale* from the early thirteenth century quotes many proverbs attributed to King Alfred, but the proverbs are not quoted directly from the twelfth-century poem *The Proverbs of Alfred* and many have no equivalent there. Alfred's name is used because it will lend authority, and proverbs are quoted because they are general and typical rather than individual. They are part of folk literature rather than of one particular work.

As we shall see in the next chapter there was a constant process of modernization at work in medieval English literary works. This can in many cases involve a process of adaptation either for new audiences or to meet the demands of new tastes. No author, not even Chaucer, was immune. The scribe of the Paris manuscript altered *The Canterbury Tales* principally by giving the language a more northerly colouring, presumably because that reflected his own dialect. The scribe of the Ellesmere manuscript altered the text for more literary reasons. He evidently felt that Chaucer had used too much alliteration in his poem, and he set about reducing the amount. At an earlier period we find two manuscripts containing Laʒamon's *Brut*. They differ so much from each other that the two versions might almost be considered different poems. In this case also we may assume that one of the scribes was dissatisfied with the poem as he found it and wanted to impose his own literary tastes upon it. With religious writings the adaptation was more often made because of the different purpose or audience to which the new version was directed. *The Mirror of St Edmund* survives in many different versions, some of which are attributable to which copytext was used for the translation, but others clearly sprang from adaptations by English authors of an existing English version. It was a work of immense popularity and it was adapted for more general or more specialised audiences, and it could be quarried by other writers to use in quite separate works. Texts were living things which could be, and were, changed to meet different needs and circumstances.

The first indication we get that a text might be preserved in its original form comes from the fifteenth century. British Library MS Additional 10340 of about 1400 contains a description of the Parson from *The General Prologue* of *The Canterbury Tales* without any further bits of the poem. The text here is so corrupt with omission and transposition of lines that it is assumed the scribe wrote the passage from memory. If so, this indicates that even if the scribe's memory was not good he nevertheless did try to commit a favourite piece of *The Canterbury Tales* to memory. Once people start to memorise texts it is a short step to quoting from them or using them in other literary contexts. Another indication of the new interest in preserving an author's words is Caxton's second edition of Chaucer's *The Canterbury Tales* (c. 1482). In his prologue to this edition Caxton claimed that an unnamed gentleman came to see him to complain of the textual imperfections of the first edition which had appeared six years earlier. His visitor suggested that if Caxton agreed to produce a second edition he would acquire his father's manuscript which contained an accurate copy of the poem so that Caxton could print from this. It has recently been shown that this story is fictitious, and so we cannot assume there were any fifteenth-century gentlemen who were deeply anxious about the textual accuracy of their copies. Caxton invented this little story to promote the sales of this edition by suggesting how much better it was than the first.[10] Even so, the fact that that accuracy could be used as a selling point shows that people were becoming more conscious of the need to preserve a poet's words in their original form.

Scribes deliberately altered the texts they were copying either to bring their language more into line with their own dialects or for literary reasons. In so doing they also made unintentional errors. Even today some passages in medieval texts defy all attempts to explain them, and these shortcomings probably arose through faulty copying. Medieval English authors expected to find mistakes in their works, as Chaucer's poem to his scribe Adam reveals:

> Adam scriveyn, if ever it thee bifalle,
> Boece or Troylus for to wryten newe,
> Under thy long lokkes thou most have the scalle,
> But after my makyng thou wryte more trewe;
> So ofte a-daye I mot thy werk renewe,
> It to correcte and eek to rubbe and scrape;
> And al is thorugh thy negligence and rape.

The interest of this poem lies in the information it provides us about Chaucer's concern for the quality of his text and also about his helplessness in the face of faulty copying. Although he was able to correct Adam's work, he knew only too well that he could not control any other scribe. Once a work was issued it became available for any man to copy; the author lost control of his text for there was no copyright. The situation with Latin texts was different. Latin was the language of the Bible, of the Church's liturgy, and of the intellectual heritage of the fathers. It was clearly essential that texts used for these purposes were accurate and indeed steps were taken to make sure they were. The universities, for example, rigorously controlled the master copies of texts which students could hire to make their own copies. Furthermore many would probably have thought it heresy or sacrilege to even attempt to improve the words of texts like the Bible. There are examples of writers taking trouble to get accurate copies of standard Latin texts. Not long after the Conquest St Anselm sent to England from Bec for a more accurate version of Bede's *De ratione temporum* (from the early eighth century) and throughout his life Anselm was very concerned about textual accuracy.[11] By contrast English literature was ephemeral, so it is hardly surprising that it was considered unnecessary to preserve an author's words in their original form.

One group of texts, those in the so-called mystical or contemplative style, stands apart in its sense of tradition from the rest of Middle English literature. Such texts include the *Ancrene Wisse* from about 1225, the various treatises written by Rolle, Hilton and the author of *The Cloud of Unknowing* in the fourteenth century, and translations like *The Mirror of the Blessed Life of Christ, The*

Chastising of God's Children and *The Orchard of Syon* from the fifteenth century. Many of these texts, particularly the earlier ones, were written for individual recipients or at least for a restricted audience. The author of *The Cloud of Unknowing* expresses fears in his prologue that his book might fall into the wrong hands and so be misunderstood. Most were works of spiritual direction and counselling which sought to guide the reader to a higher and more fruitful stage of contemplation. Although some were based on Latin, there was a strong strain of original composition in these works. What was common to these authors was the conviction that they were working within a tradition. This can be appreciated most readily by the fact that they refer to the other writings which they considered to be part of that tradition. Thus Nicholas Love in his translation of *The Mirror of the Blessed Life of Christ* writes:

> Who so wole more pleynely be enformed and tauʒt in Englisshe tonge lete him loke the tretys that the worthy clerk and holy lyuere maister Walter hyltoun/the chanoun of thurgartun/wrote in englische by grace and hiʒe discrecioun and he schal fynde there/as I leue/a sufficient scole and a trewe of all thise.[12]

Similarly the author of *The Cloud of Unknowing* refers obliquely to another book, which is almost certainly a work by Rolle, in the apparent expectation that his readers will understand to what he is referring:

> Of þeese þre þou schalt fynde wretyn in anoþer book
> of anoþer mans werk moche betyr þen I can telle þee.[13]

Such cross-references indicate that the audience for these works was relatively homogeneous, and that in its turn means it was largely associated with monastic or quasi-monastic foundations. It is known that many were preserved by such orders as the Carthusians. The monks had the facilities to keep and copy such books, and within that environment one might expect the re-reading of works which were highly valued because of their teaching. It is also within this tradition that the naming of authors seems to have been important. A large number of treatises were attributed to Richard Rolle in the fourteenth and fifteenth centuries. His name carried a certain cachet and authority on which others wished to capitalize on. Nevertheless, the existence of this tradition within a religious framework throws the discontinuity of non-mystical works into sharp contrast. It is notable, for example, that many different English translations of a single French or Latin work could be made, presumably because individual translators were unaware that translations of their text already existed. If this is so, any sense of building on the work of one's predecessors would be lacking. Nevertheless, even within the mystical tradition it is worth noting that the references to other texts are always very general. A reader is recommended to the text as a whole to follow up an idea or topic; there are no quotations from the other texts which might indicate that they were treasured for particular sayings about certain themes. The later texts can in no sense be considered as commentaries on the earlier ones which build on the work that others have done. Similarly there is no suggestion that the reader will know the words or will react to verbal echoes from these other texts. There are similarities of phrasing and imagery between texts within this tradition, but they have arisen for the most part because of the subject-matter and because of the Latin source material which is common to many of them.

ABSENCE OF VERBAL ECHO

The absence of a literary tradition as we understand it is of the utmost importance in understanding the meaning and use of words in the medieval period. Each work was written in isolation so that the words employed were without those connotations which a word acquires through its use in earlier texts. Of course writers knew and borrowed from earlier writings. Ælfric, it has recently been pointed out,[14] took over some passages from the Alfredian translation of Boethius. Thus in Boethius we find:

> Wast þu þæt þreo ðing sindon on þis middangearde? An is hwilendlic, ðæt hæfð ægðer ge fruman ge ende . . . Oðer ðing is ece, þæt hæfð fruman and næfð nænne ende . . . þæt sint englas and monna saula. þridde ðing is ece buton ende and buton anginne; þæt is God.

In Ælfric's *Lives of the Saints* this appears as:

> Ðreo þing synd on middanearde . . . an is hwilwend-lic, þe hæfð ægðer ge ordfrumman ge ende . . . Oðer þing is ece swa þæt hit hæfð ordfruman and næfð nenne ende, þæt synd ænglas and manna saula . . . Ðridde þing is ece swa þæt hit hæfð naðor ne ordfruman ne ende, þæt is se ana ælmihtiga god.

It is quite unlikely that Ælfric expected his readers to recognize where this or the other passages came from or to have any glow of pleasure from appreciating the author's reference. The words of the translation were borrowed because that was the easiest thing to do;

they were not a deliberate echo to be recognized as such by the readers. This state of affairs contrasts sharply with what a modern author might expect. If I, for instance, label a chapter in this book 'Words, Words, Words', I anticipate that my readers will recognize the allusion. When T. S. Eliot introduced modified passages from *Antony and Cleopatra* in *The Waste Land*, he risked spoiling the effect of the poem as a whole if he could not assume that the readers would immediately recognize the Shakespearian echo. Other authors are not quite so blatant in their borrowing, but even when the allusion is more concealed the author will anticipate that his reader will share his allusion – and even if he does not the editor or a critic will bring it to his attention. When Pope begins the second book of *The Dunciad* with the words 'High on a gorgeous seat . . .', the reader should recognize the echo of the opening of the second book of *Paradise Lost*, for the humour and satire spring largely from the differences in the two descriptions. Poets can contrast their own age with the past by evoking the grand descriptions of the past, as Pope and Eliot do in these cases.

The situation is different in medieval English literature. One cannot normally assume that an author intended his audience to respond to an echo created by English words. For example, it is accepted that the poet of the Old English *Andreas* knew and imitated *Beowulf*. A word which occurs only in *Beowulf* in Old English is *ealuscerwen* (line 769) which means 'a deprivation of ale' which symbolizes the terror the Danes felt at the final attack by Grendel on Hrothgar's hall. In *Andreas* there is a word which likewise occurs only there in Old English and which was formed on the pattern of *ealuscerwen*. The word is *meoduscerwen* (line 1526) which means 'deprivation of mead' and is again used symbolically in the sense 'panic' or 'dire distress'. The poet has replaced the first element of the compound *ealu-* 'ale' with *meodu-* 'mead', possibly because of the demands of alliteration.[15] If two such unique compounds containing similar or identical elements occurred in modern literature, our immediate reaction would be that the later poet intended his audience to understand the allusion to the earlier poem and that there are different levels of meaning at work. This seems improbable for *Andreas*, for the vocabulary of Old English poetry was so formulaic that audiences were not attuned to recognize echoes of this kind. The *Andreas* poet is simply taking *-scerwen* as a potential final element of a compound and modifying it in exactly the same way as he did for so many other words. Readers would find it difficult to tell which words were unique and which were simply more poetic, because there were no dictionaries and no collections of Old English poetry. The feeling that these two words are unusual is much stronger for us than it would be for them. There is also no reason to believe that *Beowulf* was so well known that the audience of *Andreas* would immediately recognize verbal allusions of this sort. That the poet of *Andreas* used the older poem does not guarantee its wider familiarity. Similarly at the end of the Middle Ages when Caxton in his prologue to the second edition of *The Canterbury Tales* describes Chaucer as 'eschewyng prolyxyte, castyng away the chaf of superfluyte, and shewyng the pyked grayn of sentence utteryd by crafty and sugred eloquence' he is copying from Lydgate's *The Siege of Thebes*. In one passage there Lydgate had written:

> In eschewyng of prolixite,
> And voyde away al superfluyte (1907–8),

though those lines are not used in praise of Chaucer.[16] Caxton had simply borrowed the vocabulary of literary criticism from Lydgate, and others were to use similar words to praise Chaucer. Though Lydgate was a well-known author, it is doubtful whether contemporaries would have seen in Caxton's words an allusion to Lydgate simply because these words were typically used in eulogies of style.

Let us consider another example. The opening line of the *Piers Plowman* B text 'In a somer seson whan softe was þe sonne' is echoed in several earlier fourteenth century alliterative poems. Thus *Somer Soneday* opens 'Opon a somer soneday se I þe sonne', and *The Parlement of Thre Ages* has a similar expression for its second line 'And the sesone of somere when softe bene the wedres'. It is quite possible that Langland knew both these poems as well as *Winner and Waster*, another alliterative poem from the fourteenth century with a comparable opening. It does not, however, follow that he expected his audience to be familiar with these poems. These other poems exist in few manuscripts and their audience was more limited than that for *Piers Plowman*. Of equal importance is that so many poems begin in more or less the same way, since this indicates it was conventional for fourteenth-century alliterative poems to open by referring to summer and the sun, just as Southern courtly poems often began with the so-called Spring setting. Where so many poems have the same beginning there can be no question that the poet anticipated that his audience would think he was imitating a particular line from a particular poem. At best the reader or listener would recognize that Langland was following a traditional pattern of composition. He would not attach importance to single words as a guide to the poet's source; he would recognize that certain words and ideas occurred together to form what linguists would call a collocational set, that is when one word of phrase automatically suggests others to speakers of that language. He would feel he was on familiar ground because he would recognize the tradition within which the poet was working; he would not seek to link this poem with any other single poem in that tradition.

Another example will add a further dimension to this question of borrowing in medieval English literature. *The Kingis Quair* (*c.* 1425) by King James I of Scotland contains a description of a tower in which the poet was held captive. Outside the tower there was a garden which he described in this way:

> Now was there maid fast by the touris wall
> A gardyn fair, and in the corneris set
> Ane herber grene with wandis long and small
> Railit about; and so with treis set
> Was all the place, and hawthorn hegis knet,
> That lyf was non walking there forby
> That myght within scarse ony wight aspye:
>
> So thik the bewis and the leues grene
> Beschadit all the aleyes that there were.
> And myddis euery herber myght be sene
> The scharpe grene suete ienepere,
> Growing so fair with branchis here and there,
> That (as it semyt to a lyf without)
> The bewis spred the herber all about.[17]

He was to see in this garden the lady with whom he was to fall in love. James I belongs to that school of late medieval poets usually called 'The Scottish Chaucerians', and there can be no doubt that his work was greatly indebted to Chaucer. This passage is an imitation of the scene in *The Knight's Tale* in which Palamon and Arcite are immured in a tower which has an enclosed garden at its foot:

> The grete tour, that was so thikke and stroong,
> Which of the castel was the chief dongeoun,
> (Ther as the knyghtes weren in prisoun
> Of which I tolde yow and tellen shal)
> Was evene joynant to the gardyn wal
> Ther as this Emelye hadde hir pleyynge. (I. 1056–61)

It was in the garden that Emily was observed by the two prisoners who both fell in love with her. What is significant about the passage in *The Kingis Quair* is that it is only a very general imitation of that in *The Knight's Tale*. There is a similarity of theme and intention, without any verbal correspondence. To us it seems that James may have remembered the setting of *The Knight's Tale* rather than the words of its description, as though he did not have a copy of Chaucer's tale beside him when he wrote his own poem. It is, however, probable that because of the reasons outlined earlier medieval English poets did not seek for verbal allusion, but thought more in terms of the imitation of themes and descriptions at a more general level. Their approach was very different from ours because of the absence of a stable tradition of English literature.

Although this lack of exact verbal repetition holds good for the whole of the medieval period, there are signs of a change towards the end. Thus the author of *The Boke of Cupide* (*c.* 1390), possibly Sir John Clanvowe, took over two lines from Chaucer's *The Knight's Tale* with which to open his poem:

> The god of love, a! benedicite,
> How myghty and how grete a lorde is he![18]

These lines are almost an exact copy of the Chaucerian lines; and the poem as a whole is full of Chaucerian language, though there are no other direct echoes. We may feel this was a direct borrowing which was intended to be understood as such by the audience. To achieve this echo the poet had to place his borrowing at the beginning of his poem in the manner of a *sententia* or maxim where it would attract most attention. This case is exceptional and stands more as an example of what happens after the close of the Middle Ages.

Contrary to what might be assumed from the foregoing English authors did recognize different styles, for particularly in the Middle English period a variety of styles emerged. Wyclif complained of the rhetorical style as compared with the plain style, and in poetry, as French influence became more marked, there developed a difference between the alliterative and what may be called the romance style. Although Chaucer wrote his works in the latter style, particularly in battle scenes he made use of the former as the following few lines from *The Knight's Tale* make plain:

> Up spryngen speres twenty foot on highte;
> Out goon the swerdes as the silver brighte;
> The helmes they tohewen and toshrede;
> Out brest the blood with stierne stremes rede;
> With myghty maces the bones they tobreste.
> He thurgh the thikkeste of the throng gan threste.
> Ther stomblen steedes stronge, and doun gooth al. (I. 2607–13)

This passage is an example of alliterative style not only because many of the words alliterate, but also because so many of them are linked together in battle scenes in alliterative poetry. Words like *tohewen, toshrede* and *threste* are found otherwise infrequently in Chaucer's works, and when they occur in isolation they rarely attract attention. Chaucer is unlikely to have borrowed these words in imitation of a particular poem; and they would have set up a general echo to the audience. Such words are part of a style and his readers would recognize them as such; individually the words were not especially significant or revealing. The emphasis on a single word was much less common then than now, and the passage would still be an alliterative description of battle even if some of the words were replaced by others which were part of the same collocational set. Similarly fifteenth-century writers who in their turn wanted to imitate Chaucer went in for a Chaucerian style rather than for deliberate echoes of his poems. For some, like Lydgate and Caxton, this meant using heavy Latin or French words as well as certain rhetorical features to suggest that their works were in the fashionable new style. Others may have tried to imitate Chaucer more closely. It has been shown that the fifteenth-century English translator of *Partonope of Blois* was 'steeped in the writings of Chaucer'.[19] This means he used phrases which we can find in Chaucer, and which became part of the Chaucerian imitations so that although there are Chaucerian echoes it is difficult to point to a particular passage as the source for an individual echo. Where the translator of *Partonope* has 'He was but yonge and tender of age' (line 1495) there are several lines in *The Clerk's Tale* which contain the phrase 'tendre of age'. None is exactly like the one in *Partonope*. As Chaucer himself used the phrase so often we may regard this example as an echo of Chaucerian language rather than a definite allusion to a particular passage. The translator wants to evoke the style of Chaucer; he does not want his readers to recollect individual passages in his works.[20]

As English was unable to provide poets with direct echoes they were forced to look outside the language for them; this meant to Latin or French. The quotations from the Bible and the Latin fathers which are strewn across the pages of medieval English texts are a reflex both of this desire to provide definite echoes and of an interest in authority, for Latin texts were preserved in their original words which consequently had significant connotations lacking in English. Perhaps typical of how this search for allusion could work is provided by John Skelton's *Phyllyp Sparowe* (c. 1505), a lament by a girl Jane Scrope for the death of her pet sparrow. This poem contains echoes from the Latin Office for the Dead, an office which had set words which would be known at least to educated people. Because the words are fixed we know immediately in the poem to what the reference is; but to do this Skelton has naturally to use the Latin words of the office. It shows that there was no English text which was so well known that its words alone would suggest what the terms of reference were. The only possible exception to this is the words of the marriage service in English which some scholars think are alluded to in Chaucer's *The Merchant's Tale*.[21] While this may be true, it seems that the English part of the service was not as standardized as most Latin services.

A recognition of this conditioning factor in medieval English poetry may modify our critical approaches to it. It will always be possible to trace a more or less direct Latin source or allusion, but not an English one since any influence from English will be at the thematic or general level. A reader cannot avoid noticing the words of the Latin office in *Phyllyp Sparowe*, but he may well feel that the connection between *The Kingis Quair* and *The Knight's Tale* is so general as to be hardly worth serious consideration in any critical evaluation. The borrowing from Latin will be so obvious that there is a danger that we today will overemphasize it to the exclusion of any English allusions. Since we have moved towards a deeper understanding of the Christian background of much medieval English literature, we may too readily assume that all English literature of this period was Latin oriented. Because it is difficult for us to trace definite influences from other English works, their general influence on an English poet should not be too readily discounted.

2

The Linguistic Background

SOME DIFFERENCES BETWEEN MEDIEVAL AND MODERN ENGLISH
Language is constantly changing and it might seem foolhardy to
suggest that there was enough uniformity in the English language
from its earliest literary manifestations in the seventh century to
the end of the Middle Ages, a period of over eight hundred years, to
warrant treating such a long period as a single unit. Within this
period there were important developments in many of the formal
aspects of the language, of which the reduction of inflections was
one of the most far-reaching and provides us with the basis for the
division of the early language into Old and Middle English. Nevertheless there is a sufficient similarity in the linguistic conditions
when they are contrasted with those operative in later periods of
English to treat this long period as a whole. Unless we understand
what those conditions were we run the risk of misinterpreting our
early literature. For it is too easy to apply techniques of literary
criticism developed for the study of more modern periods of literature, or to understand medieval English literature by using some
procedure developed for another discipline or another language,
without considering whether a given technique is suitable for the
literature being produced within the limitations of a particular
linguistic climate.

Old English was a synthetic language with a fairly well-developed
range of inflections. The point is worth emphasizing because once
we have acquired a little Old English we recognize the precursors of
many of our modern words and constructions, and that sense of the
difference between Old and Modern English begins to diminish; we
stop considering how the attitudes which speakers of a synthetic
language have towards their language may differ from our own. Yet
if we learn an inflected language like modern German we never feel,
however well we come to know it, that we grasp all the nuances
within its literature, partly because speakers of an inflected language
have different expectations. Because Old and Middle English are

rightly considered to be English and are taught at universities within Departments of English, we react to them as we react to any other period of English and fail to make sufficient allowance for the differences in outlook and expectation which may arise between speakers of a synthetic language (like Old English) and an analytic language (like Modern English). This point may be illustrated by a couple of small linguistic details which could easily be overlooked by a reader, but which together with others make Old and Middle English literature so different from what we are familiar with today.

In Old English nouns and adjectives were inflected through four cases (though there are traces of a fifth), three genders and two persons. They are also declined in what are called 'weak' and 'strong' forms. The weak and strong forms of the adjectives match those of the nouns and set up a close relationship with them. In Modern English a different pattern of relationships has emerged. Nouns and verbs have come closer together to the detriment of the relationship between nouns and adjectives. A word like *buy* may be either a noun or a verb, but not an adjective; and it would hardly occasion surprise if the noun *hat* or the verb *smash* was converted into verb or noun respectively because this type of conversion is a living force in Modern English. Adjectives, for their part, have gravitated towards adverbs so that there is a range of words which could be classified in either group. It was to distinguish these two parts of speech that eighteenth-century grammarians insisted that adverbs should end in -*ly*, though this caused some confusion in that it had originally been an adjectival ending as revealed by a word like *lovely*. In Old English, however, the inflectional patterns of the nouns and verbs were quite distinct. While it is not possible to tell from the form alone whether *georn* is an adjective or a noun in the nominative singular or whether *dæges* is the genitive singular masculine or neuter of a noun or adjective, no one could confuse the verb *gemartyrian* with the noun *martyr*, even though one is developed from the other.

In the light of these relationships let us consider a passage from *Beowulf*:

> Sona him se froda   fæder Ohtheres,
> eald ond egesfull,   ondslyht ageaf,
> abreot brimwisan,   bryd ahredde,
> gomela iomeowlan   golde berofene,
> Onelan modor   ond Ohtheres. (2928–32).[1]

(Immediately the wise father of Ohthere, venerable and awe-inspiring, meted out a return blow and killed the warrior; the patriarch rescued the bride, the wife whose jewels were plundered, the mother of Onela and Ohthere.[2]).

In standard editions of the poem *gomela* is classified in the glossary as an adjective in the weak form, for the word is common enough as an adjective; it does not occur as a noun. Yet the weak form of the adjective was used under certain formal conditions in Old English, none of which is found here. One of those conditions was that the weak adjectival form is used after a part of the demonstrative *se*, *þæt, seo*; and *froda* three lines above is correctly in the weak adjectival form. *Gomela* itself is explained on the basis that it has been attracted into the weak form by *froda* despite the absence of the necessary formal conditions which generate the weak form. It would be equally plausible and possibly more correct to classify *gomela* as a weak noun here, since it possesses all the necessary formal qualities of a weak noun and it occurs in a position in the sentence where a noun is expected. If classified in this way, *gomela* would be an example of an adjective converted into a weak noun.

To understand the implications of this case I should like to consider other examples which are less straightforward. One passage occurs in *The Wanderer*:

> Forðon domgeorne   dreorigne oft
> in hyra breostcofan   bindað fæste. (17–18)

A usual translation of these lines might be 'And so those eager for glory often firmly bind the sad thought in their heart.' In this passage there are two words, *domgeorne* and *dreorigne*, which have the normal inflectional endings of adjectives, but which occur within the sentence in positions normally filled by nouns. Modern scholars react to them quite differently. *Domgeorne*, which is in the nominative plural, is taken to be a partial conversion and glossaries usually list it as 'adjective used as noun'. *Dreorigne*, which contains the accusative masculine singular ending in *-ne*, is understood as a simple adjective referring to one of the masculine nouns in the near vicinity, usually the *hyge* of line 16, though that is in the nominative. Presumably an accusative *hyge* is understood in a kind of ellipsis. While editors give no reasons for this difference in treatment, I suspect there may be two. The first is that whereas we are familiar today with adjective conversions when they refer to animate beings, such as *the wise*, we are not acquainted with those which have an inanimate referent. Thus while we can accept 'eager for glory' as a partial conversion because it refers to 'men', we cannot accept 'sad' as one when it has some indeterminate, but clearly inanimate, referent. The second is that whereas the nominative plural of adjectives is alike in all genders and even has parallels among the noun declensions, the *-ne* ending of the adjective is distinctively masculine and distinctively adjectival; there are no nouns with that accusative form. We assume that by its use the author is principally signalling 'masculine', and hence we look for a masculine word in the vicinity. It is just as probable that he was merely signalling 'accusative'. Because neither the neuter nor the feminine is distinctive in the accusative, the author would have to use the masculine if he wished to avoid any uncertainty. Since he was forced to make a choice between three possible accusative singular forms, if he was aiming at a partial conversion he would naturally choose the form which was the most distinctive. A similar explanation could apply to *swæsne* in *The Wanderer* (line 50) where in fact there is no masculine noun in the vicinity to which it could refer. Here commentators assume ellipsis, though it is difficult to see why that is preferable to partial conversion. If *dreorigne* and *swæsne* are interpreted in this way, they would echo the use of *-ne* as an accusative marker without implication of gender which is found in early Middle English. In Laʒamon's *Brut* one can find *burh*, which is a feminine noun in Old English, qualified by *anne* when it is an object or by *þere* when it is in the dative. These forms are used because *-ne* is distinctive of the accusative and *-re* of the dative, though originally the former was a masculine and the latter a feminine ending.[3]

In Middle English the position is different in that the fall of inflections prevented the occurrence of cases like those in *The Wanderer*. But the position is equally different from Modern English in that one of the commonest forms of partial conversion in Middle English is that use of a descriptive adjective in the singular after words like *þat*; thus at line 1659 of *Sir Gawain and the Green Knight* Gawain is referred to as *þat stalworth*. Examples like this seem at first sight to resemble modern partial conversions; yet not only are they used of individuals rather than of types, but also the range of ,adjectives employed is much greater. The sense of identity between nouns and adjectives was still retained.

Some readers may feel that all I am interested in is the reclassification of certain words in modern glossaries of medieval texts. The point is much wider and involves both how we translate older texts and our reaction to them as works of literature. Because conversions of the medieval type are not available in Modern English we necessarily translate them by using some circumlocution, or by adding what we feel is the implied substantive: hence *domgeorne* becomes 'those (who are) eager for glory' and *dreorigne* becomes '(the) sad (mind)'. Although some translations make use of what is a medievalized Modern English, it would be unusual to find even there a translation like 'glory-eager bind sad in' so that modern expanded translations have a banal quality about them, which we too readily assume is a reflection of the language in the original. If we understand both these words as partial conversions the statement has a more striking gnomic quality with a very close relationship between glory and sorrow. For it would be not so much eager heroes binding their sad thoughts in their hearts as the glory-seekers binding the quintessence of 'sad' or sadness in their hearts. The difference in meaning may not be great; in poetic quality it is considerable. Similarly *gomela* in the *Beowulf* passage is a more imaginative variant of *fæder* than it is of *froda*, though here the difference in poetic range is less significant.

It is perhaps unfortunate that English still retains some vestiges of the conversion of adjectives to nouns, for those that exist seem either wooden or trite. Many, like 'the faithful', are hallowed by tradition and have the status of dead metaphors. Where we accept greater linguistic invention in conversions, it is usually of a mocking or condescending type, as in *the penny dreadfuls* or *the heavies*. How different is our attitude to conversions from nouns to verbs or vice versa. When in *Antony and Cleopatra* we come across:

> The hearts
> That spaniel'd me at heels . . . (IV xii. 20–21)

we are delighted with Shakespeare's bold extension of our vocabulary (assuming of course that *spaniel'd* is what he actually wrote). Our reactions to these two types of conversion are so different that we unconsciously accept that a poetry in which only the humdrum adjective-noun conversion is found must be of indifferent quality. We do not stop to consider what was possible at an earlier stage of the language and whether, as one type of conversion was not available to them, the speakers of the language at that time gained as much imaginative and poetic pleasure from the one type as we do from the other. We forget that Old English was not a taught language, it was not a subject of instruction in the schools. Through the analogy of Latin with its grammatical tradition, or of modern inflected languages in which children are taught the correct inflectional patterns, we assume that writers of Old English used an adjective in this type of construction only when they understood a noun to go with it. It is reasonable to suppose that the situation was more fluid and the language treated less 'grammatically' than we imagine.

The second linguistic detail I wish to consider in this chapter to highlight potential differences between modern and medieval literature has some features in common with the first. It concerns the process known as back-formation, by which a new word is formed in the language by using the root of a word already in the language as though the latter was formed from it. Thus *burglar*, a French loan-word in English, produces the verb *to burgle*, the existence of which gives the impression that in English the noun is formed from the verb. In fact the verb was coined only in the nineteenth century, though the noun has been in English since at least the sixteenth. Back-formations became very common in the nineteenth and twentieth centuries and they are one of the major ways of enlarging our vocabulary. Because such formations often have a racy and informal quality about them, like the noun *peeve* from the adjective *peevish*, we attribute qualities of linguistic virtuosity to authors who extend the vocabulary in this way, for back-formation is, as Dr Onions said, 'our favourite device'.[4]

The importance of this example lies in its indication of our present attitude to lexical creations. Although back-formation could be described as a mechanical process, examples of it are at first strange and consequently excite notice. We regard borrowings from foreign languages, like *sputnik*, in a rather different light because such words are either technical or merely useful with no element of the un-expected. A word like *peeve* attracts attention because it will occur in a context where we would expect another, more familiar word. In Old and Middle English back-formation is exceptional. The vocabulary at that period was extended by using other means such as borrowing from a foreign language or creating new compounds. Although both these methods can be found in Modern English, they are less common in works of literature, for the one is technical and the other smacks of the older poetic style which moderns avoid in their more informal style. Hence we discount the extensions of the vocabulary in the medieval period as artificial rather than imagina-tive; and this in its turn affects our estimate of the quality of the literature. In a linguistic environment in which our modern approved methods of lexical enlargement were not available it is likely that the writers and speakers of the time regarded the forms of poetic extension which could be used as pleasurable and witty. Because some kinds of linguistic inventiveness were closed to them others may have been exploited more frequently.

These two examples alone have raised several questions of wider import such as what effect the absence of formal instruction in English may have had on users of the language and what kind of pleasure one might expect from literature given the prevailing linguistic conditions. In the rest of this chapter I should like to consider the wider linguistic background and how it affected writers in their approach to literature. In the rest of the book I shall then consider in greater detail the implications of this chapter.

ABSENCE OF A STANDARD LANGUAGE

The most important feature of the English language in the medieval period is the absence of a universally accepted standard, for a standard language is a taught language. People naturally recognized that others spoke differently from themselves, and in this period there were some tendencies towards uniformity. Nevertheless without a standard language most writers were content to use their own dialect without feeling they should be using a written language which was different from their spoken variety. Another result was that works of literature were freely transposed from one dialect to another. The Ruthwell Cross contains a runic inscription of part of *The Dream of the Rood* in a Northumbrian dialect which probably dates from the eighth century. The whole poem is preserved in a manuscript probably written in the South of England in the tenth century. As a result of the move from north to south and of the passage of time, the words, the inflections and the spellings were modified to make them acceptable to contemporary audiences. The same applies to texts in the Middle English period. At no time was there a norm of spelling, inflectional usage or syntax to which writers and copyists throughout the country felt they had to adhere. The result is that many texts were written in a mixed dialect which arose either because the author used a variety of forms in his own speech, as may have been true at some periods of speakers in the London area, or because different copyists introduced new dialect forms without entirely eradicating those from an older or different dialect.

There were periods when uniformity was encouraged. Thus late West Saxon is much more homogeneous than most other Old English dialects. It has been shown that the school of Winchester tried to develop a particular style by preferring certain forms and words.[5] Similarly the language of the *Ancrene Wisse* group of texts from the West Midlands exhibits an unusual linguistic uniformity. Even individuals, like the author of the *Ormulum* (*c.* 1215), invented their own spelling conventions which they observed with regularity. However, most of these attempts were shortlived and many can be associated with a particular scriptorium or school where there was a teacher with sufficient authority to impose his own standard. The example of the *Ormulum* is significant in showing that normal written forms of the language were unacceptable to anyone who wanted to present a text in a consistent written form. Nevertheless it remains an oddity in Middle English in that it was more common for scribes and authors to use a variety of spellings within their works. An instructive example of this is provided by MS Cotton Caligula A ix in the British Library, which is a thirteenth-century manuscript of

Laȝamon's *Brut*. In this manuscript the scribe made a mechanical error of copying which led him to repeat fourteen lines of the poem which he had just copied. Although he copied these fourteen lines twice from the same copy, the two versions he produced show differences in syntax, word-order, inflection, spelling and vocabulary.[6] There is room here to quote only a few lines. Where one version reads:

> Peitreius ihate
> heh mon of Rome   Mid six þusend kempen
> þan Romanisce to helpen   & mid muchelere strengðe
> leopen to þan brutten   and lut þer of nomen
> ah monie heo of sloȝen;

the other has:

> Petreius ihaten
> hæh mon of Rome   mid six þusend kempen
> þan Romanisce to helpen   And mid muchelie strenðe
> leopen to þan brutten   and lute heo þer nomen
> ah mo monie heo þer sloȝen.

The differences are significant, if not profound.

Within Modern English the development of a standard language has meant not only that there are spellings, inflectional and syntactic patterns, and lexical preferences to which a writer must adhere if he is not to be considered ill-bred or provincial, but also that an attitude of correctness in the language has been fostered. Naturally, the standard is constantly changing, but many speakers of the modern language feel it is stable and demand that this stability be defended against all encroachments. In the medieval period change in language is a constant theme, particularly towards the end of the period when men were beginning to understand what advantages might accrue from having a standard language, for a standard was then beginning to emerge. It was at this time when men could compare the state of English with that of Parisian French that the absence of a standard would be most keenly felt and lamented. Chaucer's comments on this topic are too well known to need repeating here; but his views were echoed. A religious writer put it this way: 'Oure language is also so dyuerse in yt selfe, that the commen maner of spekyng in Englysshe of some contre can skante be vnderstonded in some other contre of the same londe.'[7] Caxton's complaint in his prologue to *Eneydos* (*c.* 1491), on the other hand, stresses how English has changed over the ages rather than the diversity among dialects: 'And certaynly our langage now used varyeth ferre from that whiche was used and spoken whan I was borne, for we Englysshemen ben borne under the domynacyon of the mone whiche is never stedfaste but ever waverynge: wexynge one season, and waneth and dyscreaseth another season.'[8] One reason which accentuated the feeling of impermanence in the language was the absence of any formal teaching of the English language, for only Latin grammar was taught in the schools. Presumably people took their own speech as their standard for writing, though this could seem very unsatisfactory to those who reflected over the apparent stability and regularity of Latin.

CONSEQUENCES OF THE ABSENCE OF A STANDARD

Within modern English the development of a standard with its accompanying insistence on correctness has brought certain consequences in its train. The first is the relegation of non-standard dialects to a lower status in the estimation of speakers of that language. Dialects cease to be a vehicle for serious literature, and dialect poetry today is considered either quaint or folksy. The second is a feeling that English is an entity which has to be jealously guarded against any debasement and unacceptable innovation whether on a spoken or a written level. The third is a rigidity which can seem to be a negative and restricting quality in the growth of the language. This has meant that spoken and written forms of the language have developed separately for it is more difficult to control the spoken level. Nevertheless there is a constant pressure to remodel the spoken language on the basis of the written forms. The standard soon becomes too limiting and teachers are satirized for their pedantic insistence on correctness. In *Love's Labour's Lost* Holofernes is pilloried for his insistence on the 'correct' Latinate etymological spellings of English words in flagrant defiance of their then usual pronunciation. This type of satire is unthinkable in the medieval period because the written forms had insufficient consistency to act as a basis for correct pronunciation. The introduction of printing enabled uniformity to spread quickly. Similar attacks on correctness are found frequently in more modern times. In *The Rivals* Mrs Malaprop exposes those who use polite, learned words to show their breeding at the expense of the shorter and commoner English words. In the late nineteenth century the cult of spoonerisms was motivated by this same reaction against hyper-correctness. These examples exhibit a desire to ridicule and to flout what were felt to be inhibiting notions of linguistic propriety, for in each case there was an element of play which comes from the absurd, racy and colloquial nature of the resulting confusion. It is hardly surprising that we should increasingly reserve our approbation for this type of linguistic innovation, and some recent writers have responded by taking syntactic and lexical dislocation to extreme ends.

Confident in the stability of our standard language with its accepted conventions and inherited traditions, we take pleasure in enlarging it by recourse to colloquialisms, slang and distortions. It is because our language is so formalized that we set store by unconventionality and freedom; we want to break away from its constrictions. The natural tendency is to look to the colloquial language which seems by comparison to be uninhibited and spontaneous. In the Middle Ages the situation was exactly the reverse. Writers of English suffered from an inferiority complex in regard to both Latin and French, an inferiority engendered by its comparative poverty and instability. Although this attitude can be most clearly seen in the later Middle English period and the Renaissance,[9] its presence can be inferred earlier from hints in extant works and from the constant reliance on translation from those languages. Far from making his written language more colloquial, an author was intent on giving it the dignity and status which he attributed to Latin and French. Colloquialism and a racy quality were the last things he wanted to create. On the contrary he relied on learned foreign words, heavy words and artificial syntax and constructions, for it was only by abandoning the colloquial that English could become elevated. The two approaches to language as a literary medium are totally opposed.

The absence of a standard spelling produces certain limitations in the written language. In Modern English our regularized orthography enables us to identify words with an unusual spelling as being colloquial, dialectal or archaic. By using spelling variants a writer can introduce a whole range of characters with different speech patterns or he can surprise the reader by using a word from a different regional or class dialect than the anticipated one. Thus such forms as *gi'me* for *give me* are used to indicate the colloquial nature of a dialogue. Nowadays such forms are less likely to imply social comment; whereas in the nineteenth century a spelling like *'umble* in the dialogue would brand its speaker as distinctly low-class. A whole range of linguistic tools thereby becomes available to the modern writer, which by the nature of his language could not be used by his medieval counterpart. As manuscripts were freely transcribed from one dialect to the next and as their language was modified or modernized accordingly, the nuances which might have been indicated by spelling were not possible. Indeed the absence of a standard probably meant that although potentially there were more markers of social and geographical origin available in the medieval period, such markers could not be used in written documents. Consequently all

43

conversations in medieval English literature have a sameness about them which we, trained as we are to look for clues as to character and status from speech, find puzzling and often attribute to a failure of poetic ability. Only very broad distinctions between polished and vulgar speech were possible; subtleties were impossible. It has, however, been suggested that many authors may have used *thou/thee* or *you* carefully to indicate how a person was regarded by the speaker, just as speakers of modern French or German distinguish the polite from the informal forms. While this is possible, the general absence of other markers and the irregularity of the use of *thou/thee* and *you* in most Middle English works indicate that contemporary writers and readers did not expect this kind of distinction in their literature. With our modern interest in such distinctions it is we who insist on finding it there.[10]

For the same reasons it was difficult to use differences in age or dialect for literary purposes. Writers could not give older characters a more archaic speech as compared with a younger man or give a churl a more dialectal speech to indicate his lack of breeding. In Old English poetry, for example, the dialect boundaries are so blurred that some scholars have suggested that poets wrote in a mixed dialect or poetic *koiné*. If so, how could they use dialect words or constructions for any purpose? It was simply not possible to give descriptions a particular character by introducing into them a large number of regional or archaic words; the writer could not distance himself from his language. It is noticeable in reading medieval literature what little use is made of different dialects or languages. The Prioress in *The Canterbury Tales* is said to speak French 'After the scole of Stratford atte Bowe', though her tale contains no evidence of this. Chaucer used too many French words in his ordinary writing to make a superabundance of French words striking. Similarly in book 10 of Malory's *Le Morte Darthur* (1469–70) we learn that 'whan sir Lameroke herde kynge Marke speke, than wyste he well by his speche that he was a Cornysh knyght', though once again there is nothing in his dialogue to pinpoint his Cornish origins for he speaks in exactly the same way as any other knight. The opposite side of this attitude to language can be studied in the interesting case of *The Later Genesis*. This poem from the late ninth century is a translation into Old English from Old Saxon, a Continental variety of West Germanic. That the Old English poem was translated was deduced by the nineteenth-century German scholar Eduard Sievers, whose hypothesis was vindicated when a fragment of the Old Saxon poem was discovered. Sievers was able to posit the Old Saxon source from a number of forms and words which occur in the poem which are unique in Old English but which are paralleled in Old Saxon. It is unlikely that the translator deliberately left in such Saxonisms to give his work a particular atmosphere or that his audience would have been aware of them. If Old English poetry was written in a mixed dialect, a few Saxon idioms would have been no more notable or significant than the other dialect words found in the poetry. The absence of any concept of a limited word stock would make it impossible to recognize which were significantly different words.

Although differences in speech were quite familiar to everyone, as these examples show, and as we know from such fourteenth-century writers as Trevisa, the representation of those features in writing was quite another matter. In the medieval period there were only two major attempts to represent a dialect different from the one used principally in the text. The first was by Chaucer in *The Reeve's Tale* where the two Cambridge undergraduates who come from 'fer in the North' use certain words and constructions which were characteristic of the north rather than the south. I am not at the moment concerned with the accuracy of the representation of that dialect, but simply with the reasons for its inclusion. The northern dialect was that furthest away from London and hence the most distinctive; that is why Chaucer used it. A dialect nearer London, such as the Midland one, would not have been noticed so readily by his audience because people were not in the habit of looking for such differences in writing. The difference in speech forms had to be at the extremes to make it remarked. While the dialect may have been introduced to add to the fun of the tale, no social comment is implied since the two undergraduates are socially far superior to the miller and his wife and ultimately get the better of them. Little would be lost if they spoke London English. It seems likely that the idea for its inclusion came to Chaucer from his knowledge of French *fabliaux* in which provincial speakers and foreigners were often made fun of because of their speech. To Chaucer it probably appeared that *fabliaux* ought to include some provincial speech, but this was an attitude which was imported from abroad rather than one which arose from the state of the language and the reactions of indigenous speakers to it.

Indeed the dangers inherent in his use of a different dialect (and the reason why none of his fifteenth-century imitators followed him) are shown by the history of the manuscripts of *The Canterbury Tales*. Of these the most significant is the so-called Paris manuscript. This was copied in the North Midlands for Jean d'Angoulême perhaps about 1430, but certainly during his captivity in England. The scribe gave Chaucer's English a northerly colouring by introducing northern words and inflections throughout the tales. When he came to *The Reeve's Tale* he sometimes kept the northern forms Chaucer had used and he sometimes altered them to the northern forms with which he was most familiar, for the scribe did not live as far north as John and Aleyn. He even transformed some of the words which Chaucer had left with a southern form into 'northernisms'. The result was that the undergraduates' language ceased to be distinctive. While not identical with the language of the rest of *The Canterbury Tales*, it was sufficiently alike not to arouse the attention of a reader of this manuscript.[11]

The other example comes from the Second Shepherd's Play by the Wakefield Master. This play may well be from the middle of the fifteenth century or later and is thus right at the end of our period. In it Mak the sheepstealer puts on a southern accent to try to fool his fellow shepherds. There is little doubt that his use of the southern dialect is an indication of the growing prestige of the standard London speech, an influence which can be traced in other fifteenth-century records. Its occurrence shows how the development of the standard would foster an attitude of elitism among those who spoke it so that they would look down on those who failed to conform. This example therefore looks forward to that great vogue in the use of different dialect and speech forms which broke out in England in the sixteenth century. Flemish speech is satirized in Medwall's *Fulgens and Lucrece* and Dekker's *Shoemaker's Holiday*; French English is a source of gentle amusement in Shakespeare's *Henry V*; and Shakespeare presents us with Welsh, Scottish and Irish speakers in that play. The 'Kentish' dialect is used as a disguise by Edgar in *King Lear*[12] and other examples from Shakespeare could be cited. Characteristic of the sixteenth century is the rise of the jest books, the earliest of which was *A Hundred Mery Talys* (1526). The humour of these short tales is built round a witty reply or remark. They involve misapplications of common expressions, puns and various forms of linguistic distortion. It is usual for dialects and the pronunciation of foreigners to be treated automatically as ludicrous. In *A Hundred Mery Talys* Welshmen and Northerners are pilloried for their language alone.[13] What a different situation from that which prevailed in the Middle Ages!

The absence of regional dialect registers in medieval English literature is echoed by the absence of argot, slang, archaisms or class dialects as markers of character or indices of atmosphere in descriptions. In more modern literature it has become customary to create a special effect by using a specialized vocabulary. For example, a description of any place in the Middle East would refer to such distinctive features as mosques because we are interested in knowing how such places differ from what we are familiar with. Consequently an author will use a vocabulary which is significantly different because the inhabitants and towns of the Middle East have many non-English aspects. In this case the author would rely on many words of Arabic origin. But a description of a castle in Middle English is unlikely to contain any distinctive regional features and it would be difficult from the description alone to know whether the castle in question was in England or France, or even for that matter in heaven or hell. If there were differences, these arose from differences in time, for new architectural features were added as time went on. Of course medieval people travelled less extensively than we do and many of them no doubt imagined that all castles looked like the ones they knew. There was anyway in medieval literature an idealizing strain which would also tend towards the removal of particular differences. The modern writer likes to be well-informed and to create original effects. He can use a vocabulary which contains old and modern language, English archaisms or even his own inventions to distance his subject and to provide it with a flavour significantly different from his readers' experience. Spenser was the first author to make use of this technique to any extent and *The Faerie Queene* reveals how the development of a standard created linguistic conditions which could be exploited only from the sixteenth century onwards.

In Spenser's case it was not only the creation of the standard which is involved; it was also the ability to preserve an author's words in the way in which they were written. The means of doing this was given a great boost by the discovery of printing. Because Chaucer was such a famous author his poetry was still read in the sixteenth century and through the rise of printing it was familiar to a wide range of people in a language which was different from that in which they wrote. Spenser could make use of that discrepancy to create a Chaucerian tone in his poem by using words that Chaucer used or was thought to have used; and he knew that his audience would understand what model he was using. The study of Old English did not develop until the seventeenth century.[14] When it was recognized as a subject worthy of study it increased the awareness of the history of English and the differences that existed between the past and the present language. These differences could then be exploited in literature so that descriptions of fairyland and the other world, for example, took on a new dimension; in medieval English literature there was no difference between the language used of human and of non-human beings or dwellings. There are advantages and disadvantages with either system. Medieval writers find no difficulty in writing about the other world precisely because the vocabulary they used was the same for that as for any other subject.

There was no straining for effect or artificiality; equally there was no sublimity. Modern writers, on the other hand, feel that the mysterious or the other world calls for special treatment and so run the danger of being either ridiculous or exaggerated.

LACK OF IDENTITY IN ENGLISH

The inability of medieval writers to use the language to distance their subjects and to present them in a language different from their normal usage arose because there was no real sense of Englishness within the language. This was only partly the result of the absence of a standard language. It was attributable also to the absence of any dictionaries of the language. Glossaries, which were principally an aid to learning Latin, are found from the Old English period onwards, but collections of all the words in the language are a relatively recent phenomenon. Such collections are intended today to describe which words are found in the language at a certain point in time, though in the past there was a more prescriptive side to dictionaries. Even today words are often included only if they are found in a written text. Consequently people feel there is a respectability about the words given in the dictionary and there is an entity 'The English Language' which has a boundary which can be clearly delimited. A feeling of exclusiveness develops. Words not in the dictionaries are felt to be interlopers whose presence is noted and needs to be justified. In a literary context it is accepted that such interlopers have been introduced deliberately for the creation of a particular effect. One might say that in modern writings such words are marked, whereas in the medieval period they are unmarked.

Naturally readers in the medieval period would respond to the presence of a lot of French words in any given text; but they would regard them as part of a general elevated tone which they would applaud. They would not seek any significance in the particular choice of French words or even notice an occasional French word within a more English section. It is also true that in some medieval texts we find references to a 'proper English'. Richard Rolle in the prologue of his *English Psalter* (c. 1338) wrote: 'In þis werk I seke no strange Inglis, bot lightest [easiest] and comunest [commonest] and swilke þat es mast like vnto þe Latyn, so þat þai þat knawes noght Latyn, be þe Inglis may cum tille [understand] many Latyn wordes. In þe translacioun I folow þe letter als mekil [much] als I may, and þare I fynde na propir Inglys I folow þe witte of þe word, so þat þai þat sal rede it, þam thar [need] noght dred errynge.'[15] But Rolle's *propir* seems here to mean no more than 'suitable' and does not imply that he felt English had a character which should not be infringed, for his whole tone suggests that for him English was inferior to Latin by which his work was to be judged.

The feeling for an identity to English was strengthened in the sixteenth century by the so-called ink-horn controversy. The dispute was between those who reacted against the excessive borrowing of foreign words and those who wanted to enrich English by further loans. It underlines the fact that people were becoming conscious of English as a language which could, and should, be purified. It indicates a desire to throw up barricades against foreign words as though there was something inside those barricades worth defending. The confidence and exuberance of the nation were reflected in the attitude to the language. From that time onwards there have been few periods which have not contained their staunch defenders of the purity of the English tongue. At first sight it might seem that the situation was much the same at certain times in the medieval period. Wyclif, for instance, insisted that sermons should be written in a simple style without elaboration. Wyclif, however, was concerned not so much with the purity of English as with the extravagance of rhetoric, and his arguments were the same as those used in the defence of Latin. He stands in the Christian Latin tradition going back to Jerome which sees in classical rhetoric a seductive opiate which can all too easily distract attention away from the basic message of the Bible. It is true that rhetoric for Wyclif involved the use of learned Latinate words, but it involved principally the use of rhetorical word-play and the arid schematization found in those sermons written to the rules of the preaching handbooks. Wyclif's writings are not in fact notable for their purity of English, even if they are less rhetorical than many written at that time.

Neither Wyclif nor other medieval writers would have understood the concept of pure English, for it is something which can arise only when a standard language has developed. To them the English language needed enriching and ennobling, and how else could this be done if not by borrowing words from other languages? In any case there were too many translations and adaptations of foreign works for a feeling of exclusiveness or purity to develop within English. Ultimately the difference between the Middle Ages and the Renaissance in England was between an age which used English for communication without worrying about the sufficiency of the language and an age which was intensely concerned about the nature of English. For in addition to the writings sponsored by the ink-horn controversy, there was in the sixteenth and seventeenth centuries a vast flood of books on all aspects of the English language; the subject generated intense interest. Rhetorical handbooks in English, pleas to enrich the language and attempts to justify innovations or

49

archaisms issued from the press. There was nothing comparable with this in the Middle Ages for Latin had too strong a grip over the minds of men.

MEANING AND GRAMMAR

The absence of dictionaries in the medieval period may have contributed to other differences in the way language was used then. Today dictionaries create the feeling that words have a closely defined meaning, and the provision of such definitions is part of an editor's task. Imagine a situation in which dictionaries do not exist. How would anyone grasp the range of meaning of a word without the literary and linguistic resources available to the modern dictionary-maker? Without dictionaries words will be only partly understood, as happens today with words from a different part of the country which are not included in standard dictionaries. The words used by poets like Hopkins or novelists like Joyce are open to a variety of possible interpretations because they are new and idiosyncratic and have not for the most part been recorded in dictionaries. The difficulty in understanding words in literature was accentuated by the many new compounds found in Old English and by the great number of loanwords from Latin and French in Middle English. The evident care taken by sixteenth- and seventeenth-century authors to explain a new word is rarely found in the Middle Ages, though some loanwords are linked in a doublet with a native word. When readers came across new words they would have to understand them as best they could; it was not possible to look a word up in a reference work, for there were none available.[16] Medieval poems which contained difficult words were not issued with explanatory wordlists as happened later in cases like Spenser's *The Shepheardes Calendar*; and it was only after the end of the medieval period that medieval poems like *Piers Plowman* acquired glosses written in the manuscripts.[17]

Probably readers grasped the general intention of a word by assessing its meaning from the context in which it occurred. This limitation might have affected the type of literature produced and the methods used by the authors. Where words are more fluid in the boundaries of their meaning, there will be a tendency not to rely too heavily on individual words to carry the main burden of the work's message. Individual words will need support through repetition, parallelism and balance, and indeed through participation in a wider context like the paragraph, which would be used as the major vehicle of the meaning. Where individual words carry less meaning than we attribute to them they will acquire significance through being associated with other words in traditional groupings or collocational sets. Such habits lie behind the use of formulas and themes in medieval literature whereby an author constructs his meaning by phrase or theme rather than by the use of key words, as might be more normal today. Our period comes before that change in philosophic attitudes characteristic of the seventeenth century which led to the closer identification of words with things. Medieval writers were used to handling words in a less rigid manner. Words were used not only to carry meaning but also to contribute to wider effects such as impressing the reader, elevating the style or creating musical rhythms. Hence medieval writing is more leisurely than ours, for readers were not attuned to the concept that every word is pregnant with significance. They would not assume that only one word was correct in any given sentence since that attitude presupposes a sharp discrimination between related words.

Nevertheless, this attitude is reflected more in writings in English than those in Latin, for the latter was the language of the Bible and of religious discussion. In this case care concerning the use of individual words was more important, and much biblical exegesis was devoted to the explication of words which had become key concepts in religious thought. There is no evidence that this approach affected the employment or understanding of words in English, though in imitating Latin writings some English religious authors do provide definitions of words. In such cases it seems as though the impetus was the wish to provide moral instruction rather than a philosophic or linguistic concern. In religious writings heresy might have acted as a restraint on the use of language and as a spur for more exact definition, but it seems not to have been an important force in England till after the time of Wyclif (no doubt because of the absence of any major heresies) and even then it came into its own only towards the end of the fifteenth century with the growing success of Protestantism. Otherwise it may be possible that the preference at the school of Winchester in the tenth century for certain words was inspired by an attempt to make English words carry the same significance as Latin words, so that there would be less chance of ambiguity and misunderstanding. But as we have seen, this attempt to achieve regularity was short-lived.

In the medieval period English was not a taught language, that is to say there was no formal instruction in English grammar or composition. The absence of this form of instruction necessarily meant that there was no concept of correct English, for correctness in language is a product of teaching. Latin was the language which was taught in such schools as existed and it was probably the language in which many learned to read and write. When in *Piers Plowman* Langland wrote:

> Grammer, þe ground of al, bigileþ now children,
> For is noon of þise newe clerkes, whose nymeþ hede,
> That kan versifie faire ne formaliche enditen,
> Ne nauȝt oon among an hundred þat an Auctour kan
>   construwe,
> Ne rede a lettre in any langage but in latyn or englissh.
>
> (B XV 372–6)[18]

he clearly thought of Latin as a language which had grammatical rules and which contained the means of formal composition. It was the centre of education and writing. As a language with a long grammatical tradition it had established rules of syntax and composition which some writers may have transferred to English. If so, it would have been in a spirit of enlargement, by extending rather than by circumscribing what was possible in English. Latin was not then the restrictive force which it has since become, for Latin is now a model for the production of a language which is regular and in which the syntactic choices are well defined. This state of affairs was achieved by applying concepts of correctness and logic, largely based on Latin, to English usage. Dryden attacked Shakespeare for his many illogical and ungrammatical expressions, and the eighteenth-century grammarians followed by formulating rules which are still generally observed even if the reasons for having them have since been brought into disrepute. Though he knew Chaucer's works, Dryden did not criticize his language, presumably because by the end of the seventeenth century Chaucer's language was so old-fashioned that no one could have regarded it as a stylistic model to imitate. Chaucer's language was so barbaric that it needed wholesale modernization, not simple correction. Why was this so?

Old English, as we saw, was an inflected language. By the end of the Middle English period most of the inflections had fallen so that English had become an analytic language rather than a synthetic one. To achieve this result profound changes in the structure of the language were taking place throughout the period. These changes were not constant or uniform over the country. Different dialects developed at different speeds: the northern ones changed quickly whereas the southern ones were more conservative. As older manuscripts were continually being modernized and as scribes were used to copying manuscripts written in different dialects, the average literate person was likely to have been familiar with a wide range of linguistic forms and expressions. It is quite likely that speech was much more mixed than it is today. People would not have used the same form or construction all the time. And as if the variety in usage resulting from the changes within English itself was not enough, the language was subjected to further disruptive influences. The Scandinavian invasions, stretching from the eighth to the eleventh centuries, resulted in a large part of the country being settled by Danes and Norwegians who spoke a language which could be understood by the English (or so later Scandinavian writers like the author of *Gunnlaugs saga* would have us believe). Yet however similar in some ways the Scandinavian languages were to English, there were important differences in vocabulary, syntax and inflections. The presence of a similar, though not identical, language led to further confusion in the minds of speakers of English as to how they should say something. It increased the feeling that there were different ways of saying the same thing. With the Norman Conquest of 1066 French became a spoken language in England and it exercised a major influence on English usage at all levels. Finally there was Latin, the language of the Church and of intellectual pursuits.

At many periods in medieval England authors and scribes were probably familiar with more than one language, at least to the extent that they copied or wrote works in either Latin or French and English. How many of us today can say this? Yet modern studies have shown that when a man is familiar with two languages, as happens today in some parts of the United States of America, his command of one language will be influenced by his knowledge of the other. If this is so now when there is a norm of accepted usage to keep deviation in check, how much more so would it have been at a period when there was no concept of correctness in usage. The bewildering variety of forms and expressions, both from English itself and from the other languages known to and used by Englishmen, would prevent a uniform usage from lasting. We may admire the language of the *Ancrene Wisse* and the *Ormulum* for their standardization, but we can see at the same time that they had no chance of surviving. In this connection we may remember that the medieval period is notable for the quantity of translation which was produced. Even today translated works often betray some of the usages and vocabulary of the language of the original work. In the medieval period this was more marked, particularly as Latin and French, the two languages principally drawn on for translation, were regarded as superior in status and hence as suitable models for imitation. Who would be able to tell whether an English or a French usage was the correct one? For example Old English *cynn* was used in the genitive in expressions like *ælces cynnes deor* 'animals of all kinds'. In Middle English this produced expressions like *what kynne tidynges* 'what kind of news'. However, possibly through the analogy of French constructions with *maniere de* it became common to include *of* after *kin*(*d*) so that phrases like *alle kynd of fishis* appeared.

The two quite different structures existed side by side. There was no attempt to banish one as ungrammatical and there were no reference books which could be consulted as to which was the 'correct' form to use. Everyone got along with the language as best he could.

3

The Editorial Process

Two aspects of modern editions of medieval texts are often overlooked by students. The first is that there is no such thing as an
authoritative text of a medieval work. It is so rare to have a
medieval author's manuscript version of his text that we may to all
intents and purposes say it is a situation which never occurs. All we
have is one or more copies by scribes who usually lived later than
and often in a different dialect area from the author himself. Modern
scholars use these copies to produce their editions, but each editor
will have different presuppositions about editing and different purposes for which his edition is prepared. Editors who use different
manuscripts for their base texts are likely to produce quite varied
editions. Similarly a text which is produced for undergraduates may
have more standardized punctuation and normalized spelling than
one intended for scholars. The amount of emendation which is
acceptable or encouraged varies from one decade to the next. So we
have this editor's or that editor's version of, say, *The Canterbury
Tales*; there is no such thing as 'the text' of *The Canterbury Tales*.
The editor's text will always be a readable text. All difficulties will
be explained and mistakes will be corrected. A modern text represents a version that no medieval reader ever read, for all manuscripts contain at least a few corruptions. A modern edition is a
medieval text seen through modern eyes, and this leads naturally to
the second aspect which needs to be stressed.

In preparing his edition of a medieval text the editor will be
influenced in his decisions concerning the many editorial problems
that arise by his own interpretation of the work in question. The
most influential critic a student reads is the editor of his set text,
whose influence is perhaps the greater because it is rarely suspected.
Thus readers of Malory's *Le Morte Darthur* have inevitably to face
the question of unity in the work because the standard edition by
E. Vinaver prints it as eight separate tales. If Vinaver had printed

this work as one instead of as eight tales, twentieth-century criticism of Malory would have been quite different. With the demise of the system of reading medieval texts by studying their textual cruces the influence of the editor has grown, for his set edition will be accepted at face value by the average student. However many critical articles suggesting new interpretations and readings a student may read and however many lectures he may attend, the words of his edition are there on the page in front of him – an insistent reminder of the editor's interpretation. One of the most important critical activities a student can undertake is to read his text in more than one edition.

A problem facing an editor is which manuscript of a text he is to use when more than one survives. Ideally it would be accepted that he should rely on the author's final version. This is rarely possible because this version does not survive in the author's holograph or even necessarily in a good manuscript, and because so many texts in Middle English and possibly also in Old English are of a composite nature. Where an author is known to have revised his text, it is still not an established practice to use the final version. Whereas an edited version of the *Ancrene Wisse* would almost certainly be based on the Corpus manuscript which represents the writer's final draft (even though it was produced for a very different audience from that of the original three noble ladies),[1] edited texts of *Piers Plowman* for undergraduate use are more likely to be based on a manuscript of the B version even though that represents neither the author's original nor his final version of the poem. A more difficult problem is presented by composite texts such as *The South English Legendary*, a collection of metrical saints' lives. This collection was modified and expanded by different authors for different purposes and localities. It is difficult to know in a case like this which manuscript to edit or even indeed whether there is such a thing as '*The*' *South English Legendary* rather than many.[2] Even where composite texts are not involved, it is clear that texts were tampered with by their readers and copyists. Caxton, for example, in his edition of Chaucer's *The House of Fame* composed an additional twelve lines for the poem which was incomplete in his copytext in order to provide it with a suitable conclusion. Similarly from a comparison with the other manuscripts of *The Canterbury Tales* it is evident that the Paris manuscript contains several spurious lines, usually consisting of an additional couplet, though occasionally they extend over eight lines. Thus *The Merchant's Tale* contains the following couplet after IV 2126:

> What lovere in this world withinne
> That castith by sleight his love to wynne?

It is possible that this and similar additions were added by Jean d'Angoulême.[3]

These two cases are very easy for us to detect; others are more problematical. They all represent what is typical of medieval English literature: changes could be made by anyone to a piece of English literature to adapt it to his own taste and purpose. The problem that this presents to a modern reader is that even if we assume an author has consciously shaped his language, this shaping would hardly survive the many changes and adaptations that were made as his text passed through different hands. This problem can be an acute one in Old English where it used to be common to exclude in modern editions those passages of the poems which were considered to be Christian interpolations in an originally pagan work. While this view could be right, it is difficult to prove and no two editors could ever agree on what parts were interpolated. It is better in such cases to start with the text as it survives in the manuscript even though it may incorporate additions and adaptations. Dr Sisam showed that the poems of the Exeter Book were gathered into a collection about the time of Alfred or slightly later and that the manuscript was copied several times before it reached its present form; it would be surprising if changes had not been made to the poems during this process.[4] Unfortunately we cannot tell what they were. All we must do in considering the language is to remember that several linguistic layers may be present in any one poem.

More importantly we should realize that an editor influences his reader's attitude to the language of the text and the effect of its individual words and phrases. I should like to give three examples to illustrate this point. In *The Shipman's Tale* the merchant uses the 'French' phrase *Quy la?* in answer to his wife's knock on the door. In Robinson's edition the passage is edited in this way:

> Up to hir housbonde is this wyf ygon,
> And knokketh at his countour boldely.
> '*Quy la?*' quod he. 'Peter! it am I,'
> Quod she; 'what, sire, how longe wol ye faste?' (VII. 212–15)

This way of editing the text may seem unexceptionable. But there are no italics in the manuscripts or in the early printed editions, so that for the first couple of hundred years at least *quy la* was not given any prominence. Today we use italics to indicate that a word or phrase from another language has not been fully assimilated into English; and this is presumably the editor's meaning in providing italics here. He wants the readers to understand that this phrase was introduced as a French expression which Chaucer assumed had not yet been adopted into the language and which he expected his audience to think of as a foreign phrase. I have already suggested in the last chapter that the concept of what was English and what was not was not as well developed in the medieval period as it is in our own. Furthermore Chaucer introduced many French words into his English works and there seems no good reason why this particular phrase should be italicized and other words left in Roman type. It is not possible for us to tell whether the status of the expression *quy la* was different from these other words, but there is no reason to suppose that it was. This arbitrary choice on the part of the editor brings with it critical implications, since if Chaucer wanted to throw the merchant's reply into prominence in this way we should naturally seek to find out what this told us of the merchant or of the narrator. By using different type in this instance the editor may both give a false impression of Chaucer's language and introduce a critical red herring.[5]

The second example I have touched on earlier. In *The Nun's Priest's Tale* the following passage occurs:

> Curteys she was, discreet, and debonaire,
> And compaignable, and bar hyrself so faire,
> Syn thilke day that she was seven nyght oold,
> That trewely she hath the herte in hoold
> Of Chauntecleer, loken in every lith;
> He loved hire so that wel was hym therwith.
> But swich a joye was it to here hem synge,
> Whan that the brighte sonne gan to sprynge,
> In sweete accord, 'My lief is faren in londe!' (VII. 2871–80).

It has been known for a long time that this passage may contain echoes of the following lyric:

> My lefe ys faren in a lond.
> Allas, why ys she so?
> And I am so sore bound
> I may nat com her to.
> She hath my hert in hold
> Where euer she ryde or go,
> With trew love a thousand fold![6]

There are two lines from this lyric which have potential echoes in Chaucer's text. The editor of Chaucer, however, has singled out one for particular editorial attention presumably because this is the first line of the lyric in the only extant manuscript. The use of the inverted commas and the capital M of *My* indicate a title. In other words the editor is asking us to accept that Chaucer referred to the first line as a title, even though the lyric has no title in the manuscript and even though no manuscript of *The Canterbury Tales* has any special marks in this line to suggest a title was intended. To a modern reader the words 'the herte in hoold' contains only a vague echo because the line is not stressed in the edition, whereas 'My lief is faren in londe' is made very prominent. To Chaucer and his audience the two would have the same emphasis, if the manuscripts are any guide. It would be surprising for Chaucer to introduce an echo from a poem before he introduced the title itself, if he was using a title, since the latter would alert the reader to the field of reference. It may be better to accept that 'My lief is faren in londe' is not a title and that the modern editor has misled the reader into assuming these words have special prominence as though they existed independently as a title. Titles of medieval works are much rarer than our modern practice of providing them would suggest, and works were referred to in a variety of ways. It was rare for a work to have a regular title which was always used to refer to it. Furthermore when an author wished to indicate a title, this was usually made clear by some kind of introductory phrase, presumably because titles were not in general marked out by special type or underlining. In *The Parliament of Fowls* Chaucer went to great lengths to indicate a title:

> This bok of which I make mencioun
> Entitled was al thus as I shal telle:
> "Tullyus of the Drem of Scipioun." (29–31).

This type of introduction is not untypical of medieval works where a title or quotation is intended. Introductory formulas like 'as the Bible says' are common enough. Where such a formula is not found, it is unlikely that a deliberate verbal echo of a line or poem was intended. In view of this two explanations of the passage in *The Nun's Priest's Tale* are possible. The first is that Chaucer did know a particular lyric, two lines from which he echoed. The second is that phrases like 'herte in hoold' and 'my lief is faren in londe' formed a collocational set within love poems. It is possible that other phrases in this Chaucerian passage were also part of that set even though they do not occur in the lyric. In other words Chaucer may have been introducing a known theme rather than a verbal echo to a particular poem. In either case the status of the words is rather different from that suggested by the punctuation in Robinson's edition, which has tended to make *The Nun's Priest's Tale* a more modern poem than Chaucer wrote it.

My third example combines features found in the other two. In the prologue of the B version of *Piers Plowman* we find the lines:

> As dykers and delueres þat doth here dedes ille
> And dryuen forth þe longe day with *'dieu vous saue, dame*
> *Emme!'* (223–4)[7]

This is a standard way of editing these lines, though it is difficult to know exactly what is intended by the choice of typographic marks. Presumably the inverted commas indicate a title or quotation and the italics imply a foreign language. In the notes to his edition, however, Professor Bennett translates and comments as follows: 'and pass the whole day . . . singing "Dieu vous save, Dame Emme"' – evidently the refrain of a traditonal song.' The way in which the notes are printed highlights the absurdity of the way in which the text is set up, for there the title or refrain is in Roman type. The notes tell us that the song is traditional, by which we must understand popular, and the text with its italics implies that the words are foreign, by which we must understand that they are unusual. Where foreign words have become part and parcel of English songs, as 'Noel' has in our modern carols, they are accepted as English and it would be unusual for them to be printed in italics. Editors of *Piers Plowman* who use italics and inverted commas here create the ludicrous situation of common labourers singing a song in a foreign language the words of which had only recently been borrowed or so it would seem. Readers might easily come away with the impression that Langland was quite out of touch with reality – and this could naturally affect their evaluation of the poem.

SOME GENERAL CONSIDERATIONS

It will be appreciated that what lies behind these three examples is an editor's attempt to come to terms with the difference between book production of our own age and manuscript production of the medieval period. Because we have so many more type faces and typographical marks than were available earlier, a modern editor is forced to make choices which can distort the meaning of the text he is editing, and a reader will make assumptions about what he is reading as a result of those choices. A modern reader expects to have a text presented to him in a way which is familiar, and the editor tries to accommodate this expectation in order to prevent the medieval text from seeming too strange. Unfortunately the less unusual it appears to him, the more incorrect assumptions based on his reading of modern literature he is likely to make. It is of course possible to edit a medieval text diplomatically or with a minimum of editorial interference, though to many this would seem like an abrogation of the editor's duty. There is a place for such editions for scholars, but hardly for students. I myself would certainly not advocate that all medieval texts should appear in modern editions with the least possible editorial intervention; it is necessary simply to be aware of what has been changed and how this affects our ideas of the language of the text we are reading. Let us then consider some of the ways in which a modern editor may subtly change the tone of his text.

We may begin with some basic considerations. One of these is that today we edit individual texts by themselves; we rarely edit them together with the other texts which accompany them in the manuscripts. We therefore think of such texts as completely independent units which exist in isolation. Where they have no title, we provide them – an action which further emphasizes the independence of a work. This is our inheritance from Romanticism. As P. M. Wetherill has noted: 'Romanticism, which is the climate in which all western society has lived for the last 150 years, stresses what distinguishes one man from another; it also attaches great importance to the world of feeling. It therefore makes the two primary aims of textual criticism possible: *to consider a text in its individual entirety and as an imaginative phenomenon (rather than as a mere collection of ideas).*'[8] Naturally because some medieval texts are all found in the same manuscript it does not follow that they were all by the same man or even that they were written at the same time (though as texts were continually modernized the question of the time of a text's composition was less important then than it may be to us). All it proves is that some scribe or collector thought them all so much to his taste that he put them into one manuscript.

In the absence of any other evidence the way the scribes reacted to the texts they copied by gathering some of them together in one manuscript presents us with the best information we have on the way these texts were understood at that time. While it is clear that many texts were written as independent works, there are also many cases where this is less easy to prove. The Exeter Book, for example, contains a whole range of Old English poetic material which modern scholars arrange as separate poems, though where the boundaries should come between these poems has not always been agreed. Even if we assume that the lines in the Exeter Book which we take to make up a separate poem and label *The Seafarer* existed independently of the collection, can we assume that contemporaries read it this way rather than taking it as part of a larger whole? That we edit and read these poems as independent works is part of our quest for the personal and idiosyncratic in composition, and it may affect the way we approach the language of such poems. Away from its companion pieces a poem may seem to have a more original and unique vocabulary than is in fact the case. The traditional aspect of the language will be undervalued. Furthermore, as we read poems in isolation it encourages us to fit them together in new groupings, such as secular and religious writing, which have no counterpart in the manuscript. This new arrangement can lead to faulty appreciation of the vocabulary in that we may associate certain words with either secular or religious works – a tendency which will limit the connotative range of a word. Or alternatively when a 'religious' word occurs in an otherwise apparently secular poem it may lead us to give undue attention to that word so that we regard its appearance as very significant. In other words editing poems in isolation may encourage us to classify words more rigorously than authors or audience would have done in the medieval period.

The letters used in medieval English texts are often altered in modern editions, but unfortunately this procedure has never been carried out consistently (as it has for example in modern editions of Old Icelandic works). The best example is provided by the texts of the fourteenth century. It is fairly common in editing Chaucer to replace þ by *th*, and to normalize the medieval forms of *u* and *v* and *j* and *i*, in accordance with modern practice. In Robinson's edition of Chaucer's works some poems which are found in what he considered to be an 'un-Chaucerian' orthography (even though we have no idea of what Chaucer's orthography was) have had their spelling freely revised to make them conform to that found in the best manuscripts of *The Canterbury Tales*. The result is that Chaucerian poetry is made to have a more modern and a more consistent orthography than that found in other fourteenth-century poems. Many standard editions of alliterative poems, such as *Piers Plowman* and *Sir Gawain and the Green Knight*, go to the other extreme in that they keep þ and the medieval distinction between *u* and *v* and *i* and *j*. This double standard can produce unhappy results in both cases. It is difficult to prevent students from feeling that the language of such texts as *Sir Gawain and the Green Knight* appeared arcane, obsolete or provincial to their fourteenth-century readers because the spelling of their modern editions appears old-fashioned to us when compared with that in Chaucer's poems. It is difficult to make them realize that Chaucer may have been an innovator linguistically. It is equally difficult to make them appreciate that Chaucer's vocabulary is medieval because the spelling of their editions seems relatively modern. They tend to overlook the medieval meanings of such words as *small*, *sad* and *danger* because they read Chaucer as a modern, as the Father of English Poetry. The language of their editions does nothing to discourage this attitude.

Each editor brings to his text his own ideas as to the most suitable versification, language and punctuation for it, though many of the older certainties are now being challenged and discarded. In the Old English alliterative metre it was thought that each halfline had to contain at least two stressed and two unstressed syllables. As it has for long been recognized that halflines with more than two stresses (the so-called hypermetric lines) occurred, it has more recently been suggested that there is no logical reason to deny that halflines with only one stressed syllable are also allowable.[9] To accept this position can have consequences for the language of the text since it will not be necessary to emend those halflines which fail to have two stresses. Even more fundamentally we assume that the Old English alliterative metre consisted of two alliterating halflines and we print our texts in lines of poetry to emphasize this state of affairs, even though in the manuscripts most of the texts are written continuously as prose. This has several effects. The first is that we today think of poetry and prose as quite separate kinds of literary creation, each with its own pleasures. The expectations we bring to poetry are different from those we bring to prose. By insisting that there are two types of creation, poetry and prose, we may force on the earlier literature a distinction which may not have existed, at least not in such a clear-cut form, for the very words *poetry* and *prose* did not come into use in English until the fourteenth century. Several texts could be printed as either poetry or prose; and some editors of Ælfric's *Lives of the Saints* (*c.* 1002) use one form, and some the other. The close connection between the languages of poetry and prose in the Old English period may thus be undermined. We today react quite sharply to a prosaic word in a poetic text, a feature found frequently in the poetry from the 1930s. Our insistence on the distinction between poetry and prose in the medieval period may lead us to look for this linguistic feature in earlier literature as well, a search which can only result in a distortion between the two forms. It seems more likely that in the medieval period there existed a range of styles rather than simply a poetic and a prose language.

The second effect is that when we print the poetic works in alliterative lines we throw into prominence those lines which are either longer or shorter than the average, and this can result in their attracting undue attention. For example, in Dr Swanton's recent edition of *The Dream of the Rood* lines 75–77 are printed as follows:

> Hwæðre me þær Dryhtnes þegnas,
> freondas gefrunon, ...
> gyredon me   golde ond seolfre.

(But the servants of God, friends, heard of me there; they adorned me with gold and silver.)

The dots persuade us that something is missing in the manuscript even though in his notes Swanton indicates that the absence of a second halfline is not uncommon in Old English poetry and may have been an accepted convention.[10] To us reading the modern edition two reactions are possible: to discount these lines entirely because they are assumed to be corrupt though the sense is perfectly clear, or to attach particular importance to line 76 because it is the only example in the poem of a line without a second halfline. As line 75 is longer than usual the brevity of line 76 is striking. It is natural for us who are used to such floutings of convention and to such rapid contrasts to think the poet attached special significance to *freondas gefrunon* because we accept that a metrical feature of this sort could be put there only for a particular reason. The difference in the line lengths is accentuated by the editor's decision to print the lines this way. If the halflines were printed underneath one another, as used to be done with Old English poems and is still done with Old Icelandic ones:

Hwæðre me þær Dryhtnes þegnas,
Freondas gefrunon,
Gyredon me
Golde ond seolfre;

or if we printed these lines as prose as they occur in the manuscript, there would be little to draw out attention to this particular line. It is important to realize how our editions direct our attention to particular passages in a poem in a way which would not have occurred in the medieval period. If we printed Old English poems in the Old Icelandic manner we might encourage readers to understand that there was a poetic rhythm without necessarily inferring that any breaks in that rhythm were significant. Alterations in the rhythm are found in later poetry, where it may also have little importance. For example the Middle English romance *Kyng Alisaunder* is written in octasyllabic couplets. However, lines 621–2 appear as:

Jt shal be a þing vneste –
Heued of cok, breest of man, croupe of beest.[11]

The last of these two lines is hypermetrical, for it would read better metrically if one of the phrases was omitted. It is quite feasible that the line is corrupt, though both manuscripts agree in having all three phrases, which represent quite an acceptable pattern. It is therefore sensible to take the line as an allowable variation in the rhythm of the poem, a variation which if we insist on regularity too much (as we are always in danger of doing by our way of printing) we may fail to take sufficiently into account.

The recent edition of the B Text of *Piers Plowman* by Kane and Donaldson provides good examples of the way in which an editor can influence our understanding of the poem and its language.[12] In their introduction they mention that many manuscripts indicate paragraphs, and it is therefore likely that the paragraphing was introduced by Langland himself. Their text, however, is printed as one continuous whole without subdivisions within the individual passus. If the poem was composed in paragraphs, though, this would suggest that Langland constructed it by an ordered progression of topics which form the structural backbone of the poem. To eliminate them suggests to the modern reader that the poem is less well arranged than it is and this in turn influences our attitude to the author and his language, since a less organized poem encourages those views about Langland which see him as an untutored genius. At the same time the absence of paragraphs may encourage us to think that *Piers Plowman* is very different from other alliterative poems of the fourteenth century. It could be claimed that since they vary considerably in length the stanzas in *Sir Gawain and the Green Knight* are simply formalized paragraphs. Our attitude towards the organization and structure of that poem is influenced by that element of formality given by the stanzas. Recent editions of *Patience*, another fourteenth-century alliterative poem, have printed it in four-line stanzas. Although these stanzas are unrhymed and not necessarily syntactically self-contained, they nevertheless give the poem a more structured appearance and hence make it seem more like *Sir Gawain and the Green Knight* than *Piers Plowman*. Would our attitude to *Piers Plowman* be different if we printed it with short gaps between each paragraph? I am inclined to believe it would, since this arrangement would indicate a poet who took more care with his composition than we sometimes allow.

More importantly Kane and Donaldson have made certain assumptions about the metre of the poem and they have used these to emend their text. Statistically there is no doubt that the alliterative line in *Piers Plowman* normally contains three alliterating staves in the pattern *aa/ax*. But there are over three hundred lines which have fewer than three staves. The question is whether these irregular lines are authorial or scribal, for scribal copying can have an impact on the alliteration, as it can on all aspects of an original. Kane and

Donaldson have made the assumption that all lines which contain fewer than the norm of three staves are scribally corrupt and they have emended them accordingly. Since for the most part these corruptions exist in all the extant manuscripts, they are forced to conclude that they were introduced at a very early stage in the manuscript tradition, probably within a few years of the B text's composition. There are two results of this editorial arrangement. The first is that Langland's verse is now much smoother and more regular than we have ever known it. The rough and irregular lines have been banished. The result is a rather different poem which must affect our ideas about Langland. The close association that used to exist between *Piers Plowman* and the sermons written in alliterative prose is weakened because the poem's style is now significantly different from the rather more jerky style found in the sermons. Similarly one can no longer assume that regularity in the metre indicates a poetic climax, since the whole poem is regular. At the same time one has to notice that the quest for uniformity in the metre has not been echoed by the introduction of paragraphing, and in this edition the editorial decisions pull the reader in opposite directions. The second is that as the corruptions entered the manuscript tradition at such an early stage, we today (if we accept the Kane/Donaldson position) are nearer to Langland than any medieval reader was. This could mean that our reactions to Langland are significantly different from those which were current in the late fourteenth century and the fifteenth century when the metre of his poem was much rougher. We may now evaluate him as no one hitherto has done. Such is the power of the editor.

PUNCTUATION MARKS

The punctuation that a modern editor puts into a text will also affect the way in which we approach its language. An example of this is provided by lines 45–6 of *The General Prologue* to *The Canterbury Tales* which Robinson prints as:

> he loved chivalrie,
> Trouthe and honour, fredom and curteisie.

But A. V. C. Schmidt in his edition of *The General Prologue* prints them:

> he loved chivalrye—
> Trouthe and honour, fredom and curteisye.

As he says in his notes by punctuating in this way 'the various abstract qualities then become not *further* objects of the Knight's "love" but rather *component elements* of an all-embracing ideal.'[13]

The way in which we understand *chivalrie* is profoundly modified by the punctuation the editor introduces. In general the punctuation of most medieval texts is much lighter than we are accustomed to and it was introduced on quite different principles. Without the formal instruction in English grammar that we now have in schools, medieval writers are likely to have been less consistent in their use of punctuation marks. Indeed there was no English punctuation as such, for the punctuation marks were borrowed with the Roman alphabet from Latin and liturgical texts. Two important facts need to be remembered: firstly not only are there far more punctuation marks in modern English, but also they have more precise functions; and secondly punctuation is now used syntactically.

Unfortunately there has been no thorough study of medieval English punctuation. While scholars disagree as to the exact function of punctuation in medieval English, they are unanimous in their opinion that it was not used syntactically. The three hypotheses which seem most acceptable are that it was used on a rhetorical, liturgical or oral basis.[14] These three are not far apart in that they indicate the three major punctuation marks (the period [.], the transposed semi-colon [⁏], and the slash [/] were employed to indicate pauses for breathing, and the three were distinguished simply by the length of pause required. Such pauses were introduced at regular intervals to facilitate declamation or even chanting. They would assist oral performance rather than help elucidate the sense. In other words the punctuation was designed to break up a text into rhetorical or rhythmical units rather than into conceptual ones. The effect would be to encourage the writing of phrases of roughly the same length which were only loosely strung together in that the punctuation did not reveal the grammatical relationship between the various parts of the sentence. This is a point to which I shall return in a later chapter; here it may be noted that each reader would be forced to make the necessary connections between the parts of the sentence himself. Naturally different readers could reach different results. The effect of the modern editor's approach is on the contrary to imply that there is only one possible meaning and his punctuation strives to make that meaning obvious to his readers. It is a pleasant irony that our age which is so keen to exploit ambiguity in its own literature should seek to limit its operation in texts of earlier ages. I do not mean by this that medieval writers were trying to exploit ambiguity, but simply that their punctuation would have allowed their audiences to understand what they had composed in rather diverse ways.

As I have already indicated there were in the medieval period only three main marks of punctuation used in England: the period, the transposed semi-colon, and the slash. They all indicated pauses, with the period the longest and the slash the shortest. Not all three marks were used by every writer, and it was also possible to combine them, though whether such combined marks are significant is difficult to say. What we do not find in the medieval period are all those marks which we today take for granted, such as the question mark, the exclamation mark, the colon, apostrophes, brackets, dashes, inverted commas, and so on. Several important considerations arise as a result of this poverty. Consider, for example, this quotation from Chaucer's *The Knight's Tale*:

> Ful blisfully in prison maistow dure, –
> In prison? certes nay, but in paradys! (I. 1236–7).

In the second line there is a clear contrast between *prison* and *paradys*. In modern English punctuation the sense of surprise and shock that the repetition of prison evokes for Arcite is expressed through the question mark. In Chaucer's time there was no question mark and so he was forced to emphasize Arcite's reaction through the introduction of the phrase *certes nay but*. To us this phrase may carry with it the overtones of medieval tautology and cliché, since we may well feel that 'In prison? No, in paradise!' would have been sufficient. This feeling arises in part because *our* punctuation makes *their* language seem long-winded. Modern dismissals of medieval style as too cliché-ridden fail to pay sufficient regard to this feature of their composition. One may also note in passing that in this edition the *certes* is not given a capital though it follows a question mark. This may encourage some to think that Chaucer was here writing in an informal, or more colloquial, style, since this would be the message implied by this punctuation in modern English. Nothing could be further from reality, since the Chaucerian piece is relatively formal in its poetic construction.

Another example, also from *The Knight's Tale*, may help to drive this point home. In the line already commented on in an earlier chapter:

> The god of love, a, *benedicite!* (I. 1785),

the *a* fulfils the role of the exclamation mark in modern English. Theseus apostrophises the God of Love and wishes to emphasize his amazement at the god's power. A powerful expletive is called for, supplemented by a less powerful one to lend additional weight and emphasis. The *a* is not included simply to complete the number of syllables in the line. Because in this edition we have both an exclamation mark and italics, the *a* is left with no meaningful role and

therefore appears to be redundant. This stylistic impropriety is our
fault, not Chaucer's; our punctuation may lead us to misinterpret
his language.

It is likely that there is a connection between the paucity of
punctuation marks and the tendency towards co-ordinate sentence
structure in medieval English writings, though whether the latter is
the cause or effect of the former is more difficult to determine.
Other languages which contain a full range of subordinating conjunctions together with distinctive word order in subordinate clauses,
and a recognizable subjunctive mood, could develop subordination
relatively easily. In Middle English in particular the loss of distinctive subjunctive forms and the trend to establish a subject–verb–
object order for all clauses made it difficult to indicate subordination
unambiguously. Modern English has overcome this difficulty by
using a syntactical punctuation and by developing a wider range of
subordinating conjunctions. If medieval English had had a different
kind of punctuation, it might have been able to develop a greater
degree of subordination. Only those authors who attempt to follow
the spirit of Latin composition like the author of *The Cloud of
Unknowing* (*c.* 1375) or those who in their translations keep close to
their originals attempt any significant amount of subordination. But
even with modern punctuation *The Cloud of Unknowing* remains a
difficult text to read, not because of its vocabulary but because of
its syntactic complexities; while those who translate slavishly from
French, like Caxton, are often criticized for their obscurity.

In fairness to Caxton and others it must be stated that modern
punctuation often makes their style seem jerky and unsophisticated.
In a book of selections from his work, I punctuated a sentence from
his *Reynard the Fox* (1481) in this way:

> Also it is lityl worship to hym that hath overcomen a man
> thenne to slee hym; it is grete shame; not for my lyf, thaugh
> I were deed that were a lytyll hurte.[15]

In the original the sentence reads as follows:

> Also it is lityl worship to hym that hath ouercomen a man/
> thenne to slee hym / it is grete shame / not for my lyf / Thaugh
> I were deed / that were a lytyll hurte.[16]

Caxton did not use the transposed semi-colon. He did use a small slash,
which appears to have indicated a smaller pause than the longer
slash. His three marks are in descending order of length of pause:

the period, the slash and the small slash. Bearing this in mind we can see that his punctuation provides us with three sentences, each consisting of two clauses. The result is a series of balanced sentences, which in Caxton's punctuation makes good rhetorical sense. In trying to make grammatical sense out of this passage for the modern reader, I have distorted his meaning and given a false impression of his style. Our punctuation encourages us to put grammatical and syntactical meaning first; that was not the case in the medieval period. Style and methods of composition were therefore bound to be different.

An important aspect of our insistence on a grammatical sentence as the basis of punctuation is that it may lead us unwittingly to think of medieval literature as primitive, because it fails to conform to our standards of grammatical expectation. In *The Later Genesis* this sentence occurs at lines 368–70:

> Wa la, ahte ic minra handa geweald
> and moste ane tid   ute weorðan,
> wesan ane winterstunde,   þonne ic mid þys werode—
> (Alas, if I had freedom of action and could escape for a time,
> even a brief hour, then I with this force.)

Because the sentence contains an incomplete final clause, it seems clumsy to us and this affects our attitude to the author's style. However, it was not uncommon in Old English for a sentence to have a subordinate clause with no, or at best an incomplete main clause. Our punctuation reinforces our idea that all sentences in early texts should be grammatically complete – 'grammatically' as we understand that word – even though the sense is readily intelligible. Interestingly enough this is not something we expect from later literature and Shakespeare's use of unfinished syntactic units in his sonnet 129 has been justly praised.[17] Perhaps the author of *The Later Genesis* intended a literary effect here which we may overlook because of our insistence on grammatical propriety. We today associate incomplete or ungrammatical sentences with an informal or colloquial style, and there is a danger that we may seek to excuse 'grammatical lapses' in medieval authors by assuming they were also indulging in colloquialisms. If their standards of syntax were different from our own, this would not be a correct inference. The importance of this passage from *The Later Genesis* is that it suggests modern punctuation may not be suitable for medieval texts.

This claim may seem a little stronger if we consider a short sentence from *Le Morte Darthur*:

Than sir Palomydes, that was one Arthurs party, he
encountird with sir Galahalte, . . .[18]

Here the subject, Sir Palomides, is repeated in the *he*; and this
repetition is a common syntactic feature of Middle English texts. In
Modern English punctuation the commas marking off the relative
clause describing Sir Palomides make it quite clear that he is the
subject of a verb which is yet to come so that the *he* seems unnecessary and clumsy. With a longer relative or other kind of intervening
clause (and parenthesis is a common feature in Malory), the grammatical relationship can still be made quite unambiguous through
the use of modern punctuation marks, either commas, brackets or
dashes. Without such punctuation the meaning might easily become
confused and hence the repetition of the subject would be desirable.
It may be that certain syntactic features (even though borrowed
from a foreign language) were developed in English precisely because
medieval punctuation was light and often ambiguous, for it was not
designed to explain the grammatical relationship of the parts of a
sentence. By using modern punctuation which seeks to eliminate
ambiguity we make the medieval text seem either stilted or naive.
Their syntax is not our syntax, but our punctuation proceeds on the
basis that the two are the same for it is very difficult for us to escape
from our own prejudices and expectations in this matter.

The introduction of inverted commas into medieval texts can also
produce misunderstandings. The absence of this particular mark of
punctuation meant that direct and reported speech were less sharply
differentiated then. To some extent this still remains true and there
are situations in which we are uncertain whether to use inverted
commas or not. When a man is talking to himself, his words may or
may not be put within inverted commas. Indeed, one wonders
whether the development of such a stylistic phenomenon as *le style
indirect libre* came about because of the straightjacket forced on
written language by the use of inverted commas. For this allows for
comments which are ostensibly part of the narration to be expressed
in the words associated with one of the characters in the work, and
hence they express his views in an indirect way. Not only does this
stylistic trick provide variety, it also helps to break down the rigid
barriers between direct and reported speech. There was no place for
le style indirect libre in medieval English because the characters all
spoke in a stereotyped language which was usually the same as that
used for the narration. It was also hardly necessary, because without
the use of inverted commas it was difficult to tell what was and
what was not direct speech. Certainly scribes are known to have
inserted or omitted the occasional "X said" formula in the process

of copying, and there can be no doubt that this reflects the attitude
of contemporary readers in that each one probably interpreted what
was direct speech quite differently. After all modern scholars cannot
agree where to insert inverted commas in medieval texts. Thus
A. V. C. Schmidt punctuates two lines from *The Canon's Yeoman's
Tale* as follows:

> Som seyde it was long on the fyr making,
> Som seyde, "Nay, it was on the blowing."[19]

It is not quite certain why he has edited the lines thus, and most
editors do without inverted commas here. Probably if they had
bothered to think about it at all, medieval readers would have taken
both lines as either reported or as direct speech. To take each line as
a different form of speech may make modern readers react in a way
which is quite unnecessary. We may feel that Chaucer was being a
little fussy, or alternatively that there is some meaning which is not
immediately apparent.

Because there was an overall similarity within the language of a
medieval text, there was little to distinguish direct from reported
speech or either from authorial comment and narration. The result
was that where an author felt speech to be important, it had to be
indicated clearly. This is why in *The Battle of Maldon* (*c.* 1030) each
speech is introduced by elaborate formulas indicating the summoning
to attention by brandishing weapons. The views expressed by the
individual warriors are reasonably uniform, but the author has tried
to distinguish each individual Englishman partly by naming him
and partly by indicating his social standing. The speeches are important for the poet and so they have to be introduced deliberately by
the heavy use of formula. *The Battle of Maldon* is in this particular
very different from such poems as *The Seafarer* and *The Wanderer*.
Much critical ingenuity has been expended in deciding where the
inverted commas in these poems should be and even how many
speakers there are. This is a problem for us today and it has arisen
simply because of our punctuation, for the inverted commas have to
be placed somewhere. In *The Wanderer* the poet has made his
character very shadowy. Unlike the warriors in *The Battle of Maldon*
the wanderer has no name, no geographical home, no named lord,
and so on. He is a type who remains totally removed from any
attempt at individuality. Consequently his views as a shadowy
stereotype cannot be distinguished, and were not meant to be distinguished, from those of the author. It therefore seems immaterial
where his 'speech' ends and where authorial comment begins. His
speech embodies a general experience, and the author comments on

that general experience – either in his own person or in the role of his straw figure. After all, medieval authors frequently refer to common opinion or inherited wisdom in the form of proverbs or accepted authorities. While it is possible to put such opinions in inverted commas, such punctuation could give a misleading idea of how medieval works were composed. They used common ideas because they were common, not because they were associated with a particular authority. So much of what medieval authors wrote was traditional, that to distinguish what is a character's, his own or his predecessors' opinion, seems often pointless and misleading. Medieval writers were not intent on individualizing to the extent that we are.

Another effect of introducing inverted commas into medieval texts is that passages of direct and reported speech alternate very rapidly. A well-known example occurs in the Cynewulf and Cyneheard annals in *The Anglo-Saxon Chronicle*. At the other end of the medieval period it is a frequent feature in Malory's *Le Morte Darthur*. This alternation can make medieval writing very jerky. To avoid this jerkiness some editors emend, though this may well appear a drastic solution to a problem that we moderns have created with our own punctuation. Thus Vinaver in his edition of *Le Morte Darthur* punctuates two sentences as:

> Than sir Bors lenyd uppon hys beddys syde and tolde sir Launcelot how the quene was passynge wrothe with hym, 'because ye ware the rede slyve at the grete justes'. And there sir Bors tolde hym all how sir Gawayne discoverde hit, 'by youre shylde' that he leffte with the Fayre Madyn of Astolat.[20]

D. S. Brewer, however, has decided to edit the lines this way:

> Then sir Bors leaned upon his bed's side and told sir Lancelot how the queen was passing wroth with him, 'because ye wore the red sleeve at the great jousts.' And there sir Bors told him all how sir Gawain discovered it, 'by your shield that ye left with the Fair Maiden of Astolat'.[21]

Brewer has emended the Winchester manuscript *he* to *ye*, and in this he follows Caxton's edition. It is probable that he did so because he decided that variation from direct to reported speech should be in units of not less than a clause; and by his emendation he is able to make the second sentence parallel in its stylistic impact with the first. But Malory may have intended to stress the 'by youre shylde' or he may simply not have worried about variation between direct and reported speech even at a phrasal level. In either case Dr Brewer

may be doing less than justice to Malory by misleading his readers
as to the tone of his author's prose.

It is often suggested that the rapid alternation between direct and
reported speech is indicative of oral composition.[22] Since this feature
occurs in so many medieval English texts which were translated
from French this view seems unlikely. At least while it remains
possible that the alternation may have originated through oral composition, its occurrence in medieval texts cannot be used as proof
that they were orally composed or even necessarily composed for
recitation. For the variation is something that one notices only with
modern punctuation, and that seems an unsatisfactory basis on
which to build such an important hypothesis.

COMPOUNDING, CAPITALIZATION AND TYPE

Editing involves far more than simply putting modern punctuation
into a medieval text. Let us consider the following examples from
line 1931b of *Beowulf*, the manuscript of which reads *mod þryðo
waeg* as three separate words. Modern editors assume that only one
meaning should be obtained from these lines, but the resulting readings are varied in the extreme. Some take *modþryðo* as one word,
either as the name of the queen or as a common noun with the
sense 'arrogance'. Others read the three words separately, and in
this case *þryðo* can be understood as a proper or a common noun.
The editor is forced on account of his punctuation to make a single
choice which he must then defend. A reader of the manuscript (or
even a listener to an oral performance if there were any) would not
be in quite the same position. He would be able to take whichever
reading suited him best or fell in with his own ideas of what the
poem was about. The two aspects of this example, compounding and
capitalization, could perhaps be developed further.

To us it seems that medieval scribes were cavalier in their attitude
to word division. Partly no doubt this is because they were less
attuned to the concept of words as entities, for they had no dictionaries which seek to list all words in the language. It is only when
words are organized in this way that word division or where and
how to list any one word becomes important. We have become more
pedantic in our attitude to word division, and even hyphens now
are used much more commonly than they used to be. The desire to
avoid ambiguity has been one of the most important factors in this
development, for we would think there was a big difference between
a 'large blackbird' and a 'large black bird'. Medieval authors and
readers cannot have regarded this distinction as so important, for in
many cases they would not have been able to tell exactly which one
was meant. We have even been reintroduced to this type of ambiguity

through newspaper headlines in which a string of adjectives and nouns can appear without the grammatical connection among them being expressed. A phrase like *Power strike gamble* is one that could readily occur. In cases like this we understand the general meaning without necessarily being aware of the grammatical relationship of the three words. Possibly this is how readers of Old English, for instance, reacted to the noun strings in their literature. If so, modern editors may be mistaken in trying to reduce the general level of meaning to a more specific one. Furthermore we often feel a glow of satisfaction in teasing out the linguistic puzzle represented by *Power strike gamble* and this again is a factor that might be taken into account in deciding how contemporary audiences reacted to a half-line like *mod þryðo wæg*.

Capitals were of course found in most medieval scripts, though they were not employed on any regular basis by the majority of the scribes throughout the medieval period. Proper nouns could be with or without them, and as sentences were less clearly defined there was little occasion to introduce capitals as the mark of a new sentence. Today proper nouns have initial capitals. This presents a problem to an editor because of the frequent use of allegory in medieval literature. *Piers Plowman* provides a good example, for in this poem abstract concepts like love, peace, meed (i.e. reward), false(hood) and simony are personified. Although some examples of love, for example, are clearly intended to be the personification and others equally clearly the abstract noun, there are a great many which fall in between and could with justification be attributed to one or the other. Where there is a system of punctuation which does not discriminate so sharply between proper and common nouns, a reader can take each occurrence of a word like love to be whichever he pleases or indeed to mean both at once. For where a choice is not required, it may not be made at all. So to a medieval reader the distinction between *love* and *Love* may have been small or even non-existent. This may help to explain why various forms of allegory are so common in medieval English literature. In the *General Prologue* of *The Canterbury Tales* it is quite possible in view of the frequent personification of nature by Chaucer that many of his contemporaries understood the *nature* of 'So priketh hem nature in hir corages' (I. II) as the goddess even though most modern editors have a small *n*. Similarly in the Heremod digression in *Beowulf* (lines 901–15) a modern editor is forced to choose whether to put a capital *E* to *eotenum* (line 902) or not. He must decide which interpretation to follow, though the medieval scribe did not have to make that choice. Our punctuation may force the language of a medieval text to be more rigid than it was intended to be.

75

This aspect of capitals is very closely linked with the use of different type. Although scribes were often familiar with different scripts and had ways of indicating a special word or passage by the use of a different coloured ink or underlining, these expedients were used sparingly and in certain recognized places such as chapter headings. Today printed books make use of a large range of type and they allow us to indicate a subtle range of diversity in the language of a book. This diversity we extend to medieval works. At *Piers Plowman* B.V. 449–50 Professor Bennett punctuates as follows:

> 'Repentestow þe nauȝte?' quod Repentance; and riȝte with þat
>   he swowned
> Til *Vigilate* þe veille fette water at his eyȝen.[23]

Here *Vigilate* is both given an initial capital and put in italics. It is therefore regarded as similar to Repentance in being a personification, but unlike it in being considered a loanword. It is assumed to represent an echo of the passage in Matthew 26:41 *Vigilate et orate . . .*; and *Vigilate* is hence a personification of watchfulness. However, the use of italics implies that the medieval reader would also understand this as a Latin word which occurred in a particular biblical context rather than a word which had been anglicized and extended to a more general frame of reference. This means that the reader would understand Repentance and *Vigilate* as different types of personification. Because of the absence of any real sense of English and foreign words, I find this view unlikely.

Further examples of this kind occur throughout *Piers Plowman*. Later in the same passus the following lines occur in Bennett's edition:

> And knowleched his gult to Cryst ȝete eftsones,
> þat *penitencia* his pyke he shulde polsche newe
> And lepe with hym ouer londe al his lyf-tyme,
> For he had leyne bi *Latro*, Luciferes aunte. (481–4)[24]

The italicizing of *penitencia* again suggests that this is a foreign word which was known to be a new introduction into English; otherwise, it might be implied Langland would have used *penitence*. In fact *penitence* appears not to have been used in the poem, although it occurs in English texts from the twelfth century. It was never a very common word and it naturally occurs principally in penitential texts. Hence *penitence* (the French form) may have been just as much a learned word of restricted meaning as *penitencia* (the Latin form); it is doubtful whether the average person would have discriminated between them. Langland's usual word is *repentance*, as the previous quotation showed. As far as we can tell Langland's use of *penitencia* was not intended to carry an allusion to a particular Latin quotation or penitential passage; in itself it seems no more or less significant than *penitence* would have been. Hence we may question whether it was intended to have the significance that the italics imply. At the same time we may note that the use of italics for words like *penitencia* is taken over by editors from books on language like this one rather than from modern poetry. T. S. Eliot, for example, does not necessarily use italics for the words taken from other languages in *The Waste Land*, and few modern poets would use italics to call attention to a word borrowed from another language. Consequently the use of italics in medieval texts may make them unnecessarily learned and pedantic; it may even lessen their appeal as poetry.

The italicizing of *Latro* in this passus has much in common with *Vigilate* except that like *penitencia* it appears not to refer to any particular Latin text. There seems no reason to have *Latro* here rather than, say, *Thief* or any other English word unless Langland was forced by the demands of the alliteration to find a word beginning with *l*. If this is so, then the fact that the word happened to be of Latin origin is immaterial. As it happens the word is conveniently placed next to *Lucifer*. In Bennett's text *Lucifer*, though also of Latin origin, is not italicized. The reason is that *Lucifer* is presumably accepted by the editor as an anglicized word whereas *Latro* is not, on the grounds that this is the only time the latter occurs in an English text. The frequency of occurrence of a word of foreign origin is something that we can judge much better than a medieval audience; it is not something to which they would have given much attention. Because the word is put in italics in modern editions, we think it has some significance and make a search to find out what it is. Thus Bennett in his notes tentatively suggests that Langland may have had in mind the *latro* of Luke 23. I would suggest that our search for significance of this kind may be misplaced; we should not expect to find it in every word of foreign origin.

CONCLUSION

When we read a medieval text in a modern edition, although it is ostensibly the work of one man it is in effect the cumulative result of the labour of all early editors. Although it might seem that a modern editor and a medieval scribe were working for the same end, to make the text intelligible to their own age, their basic approach is different. The scribe is intent on the general meaning of the work without too much concern about retaining the original features of linguistic usage: the editor starts with the assumption that the words are sacrosanct and that the meaning has to be extracted from them. In medieval manuscripts there are many cruces or passages where the meaning is difficult to understand. A medieval scribe who noticed this would simply rewrite the passage in the way that seemed best to him, which is why the intelligent scribes produced the least useful texts for modern editors: their language is furthest away from the original. A modern scholar will try to see how the misunderstanding arose or to tease some sense out of the words in the manuscript.

Editing in modern times is a continuous process; when we read a text we have access to the efforts of all previous editors in trying to understand difficult passages, and these difficulties remain constant. The scribe is faced with new problems because what seemed clear to his fellow scribe twenty years earlier may no longer seem so to him; there was no memory or continuity in copying. Indeed his predecessor may have made new mistakes in his copying or in trying to correct the passages he himself failed to understand. When we read an edited text there will be few, if any, passages of unintelligible non-sense, because in the last resort an editor will emend. There will also be notes to explain the difficulties, allusions, parallels, and associated problems. We shall even know which words are traditional and which are new in so far as the extant corpus is concerned. The medieval reader would be in a very different position. It is of course impossible to tell how he reacted, though we can gain some idea from the way in which scribes behaved. So far scholars have tended to consider the role played by scribes only as it concerns the relia-bility of a manuscript; but they also provide a good indication of how people at that time approached their literary works.

Although it may be no more than a theme when an author invites his readers to correct his work, its common occurrence does suggest that authors expected their work to be changed. It is a theme that occurs frequently. Chaucer used the theme, for his reference to Gower and Strode in *Troilus and Criseyde* was a request for correc-tion, and so did Caxton. Scribes took advantage of this invitation, and presumably other readers did as well. In general the efforts of scribes were directed to making the text they copied less unique and more traditional. They rarely considered what was appropriate for a particular author or text. Thus the editor's tool of *difficilior lectio* (whereby when two manuscripts present variant readings the more difficult is likely to be the original one) presupposes that what scribes found personal, irrational or unusual they would emend to what was in their eyes more acceptable. It would be foolish to deny

that the average reader behaved in the same way. This meant that
he followed the general drift of a paragraph or section without
worrying too much about the individual words used which he would
expect to fall into certain categories. If a reader came upon a crux
he could either disregard that clause or sentence or try to make
sense of it by substituting a more traditional expression which he
thought would be suitable for the sense of that section. He would
think perhaps in themes rather than in words. Attention to the small
details of language is hardly likely to have been a feature of medieval
reading habits.

The point is worth stressing because the picture of a scribe
laboriously poring over his manuscript and copying it word by word
might suggest he took infinite pains in comprehending each word.
This does not seem to have been the case. Copying was tedious and
evidently often hurried over; it is difficult otherwise to account for
the many imbecilities which are found. The attitude can be better
shown from translation, which represents a parallel behaviour. Here
again we see lack of attention to detail. Thus the translator of
Partonope of Blois can turn the French *a Gisours* (a place name) into
Agysour (a personal name) without worrying about the meaning of
the sentence. The same applies to Caxton's translations.[25] Examples
like this could be multiplied and are paralleled by scribal copying.
Our way of reading a text is prepared and shaped by the editor, who
has spent a long time in thinking over individual words and the
meaning of difficult passages. The use of all the various typographical
devices available to him smooths our path and makes the understanding of medieval texts a very different experience from that of
the medieval reader.

4

Words, Words, Words

CONNOTATION AND DENOTATION

In this chapter I would like to review the medieval writer's attitude towards words, without worrying for the moment about the grammatical or syntactic framework into which the words fit. Today many creative writers choose their words for their evocative quality, and this is a method of composition we take to be characteristic of all ages. Hence modern critical accounts of medieval literature often pick on the evocative quality of its words. As part of this emphasis it is customary to talk of both the 'denotative' and 'connotative' meaning of words. Broadly speaking, we could say that the former is the dictionary definition of a word, and the latter is the associations which a word carries with it among the speakers, or a group of speakers, of the language. What we need to find out is whether this distinction is a useful one for medieval English literature, since the strength of modern poetry is often thought to reside in the exploitation of connotative meaning.

For the medieval period there are two problems linked with this distinction. In the first place, since there were no dictionaries to define the meaning of words and since, particularly in Old English poetry, many words were created for a particular poem, the boundary between connotation and denotation was much more ill-defined then, or even non-existent. If, for example, in alliterative poetry a variety of words was used to overcome the constraints of the metre, for the necessity of having three alliterating words per line does impose a considerable constraint on the poet, the words used may have been felt to be vaguely 'poetic' without otherwise having much evocative quality as we understand it. Their connotative force would be slight. In the second place, if we do make the assumption that words were used evocatively then, how can we recover these evocative associations? The small amount of literature which survives, particularly from the earlier part of the period, and the absence of a coherent and consistent tradition within the period as a whole are important considerations. The fragmentation of the literary output in the manner outlined in the first chapter would inhibit the development of literary connotation as we understand it now. On the other hand, the distance of the medieval period from our own prevents us from acquiring any idea of what the colloquial or at least the less literary associations of words were. There are no contemporary pamphlets or newspapers to fill in this gap for us, and the letters which are extant come from the end of the Middle English period and are apparently influenced in their choice of vocabulary by current literary conventions. Furthermore there is no evidence that writers used words of different registers in their works to create shock or to exploit the different connotations which a word had. Scribal copying would inhibit this kind of lexical use. It is true that Chaucer in *The Manciple's Tale* has the following comment on the status of words:

> And so bifel, whan Phebus was absent,
> His wyf anon hath for hir lemman sent.
> Hir lemman? Certes, this is a knavyssh speche!
> Foryeveth it me, and that I yow biseche.
>   The wise Plato seith, as ye may rede,
> The word moot nede accorde with the dede.
> If men shal telle proprely a thyng,
> The word moot cosyn be to the werkyng.
> I am a boystous man, right thus seye I,
> Ther nys no difference, trewely,
> Bitwixe a wyf that is of heigh degree,
> If of hir body dishonest she bee,
> And a povre wenche, oother than this –
> If it so be they werke bothe amys –
> But that the gentile, in estaat above,
> She shal be cleped his lady, as in love;
> And for that oother is a povre wommman,
> She shal be cleped his wenche or his lemman. (IX 203–20)

Here it appears that Chaucer is informing us that in medieval times *lady* and *lemman* had different connotations. What is significant about the passage is that Chaucer has to go to such lengths to make his point. In this case *lemman* has become marked not because it belongs to a different register, but because Chaucer has pointed to it as being a 'low' word. In the medieval period it is used in love poems and it is unlikely, despite what Chaucer says, that readers would have paid much attention to the word unless he had directed them to do so. It would be difficult for us to be certain from the extant literature of the status of *lemman*.

NATIVE CONNOTATION

In medieval literature it is possible to think that there are two major sources of connotation, which I shall call 'native' and 'foreign'. The former refers to potential associations inherent in words because of their Germanic pagan links, the latter to the associations which learned loanwords bring in their train. Because of the apparent hiatus in composition between Old English poetry and the poems of the Middle English Alliterative Revival which led to a different vocabulary being used in each period, native connotations for words in Middle English are difficult to detect. So to consider the possibility of native connotation it is better to take the Anglo-Saxon period. It is closer to the Germanic background in time, and its literature seems to spring from a more unified cultural tradition than that from the Middle English period. Unfortunately no Germanic literature prior to the Anglo-Saxon period survives. All we have are references to composition among the Germans by such classical writers as Tacitus and some early runic inscriptions like that on the golden horn of Gallehus which are written in an alliterative metre. Neither provides us with any insight into the vocabulary which might have been used by Germanic writers. Other Germanic poetry is of no help, for the alliterative poetry found among the continental Germans was introduced by Anglo-Saxon missionaries and the language of the early Scandinavian poetry shows significant differences from that of the Old English poems – differences which suggest that if there were any common Germanic lexical features they were obliterated or obscured before the onset of writing in England and Scandinavia.

We are left to fall back on individual words which may have connotations. Many of the words used in Old English poetry are of Germanic stock and as such they may have carried pagan heroic connotations with them. The difficulty is proving that they did. In the nineteenth and early twentieth centuries it was widely believed that Old English poetry was essentially Germanic and heroic in spirit so the words of the poems were interpreted as though they carried pagan connotations. This view was accepted rather than proved. Nowadays, as more and more scholars accept that Old English poetry is Christian and monastic, pagan connotations for Anglo-Saxon words are replaced by Latin ones. As already indicated in an earlier chapter it is easier to prove a Christian Latin association than a pagan heroic one, partly because of the nature of the Latin language and partly because no pagan Germanic poetry survives. That there were words with pagan heroic associations still remains possible, even if it cannot be proved. The problem of identifying these associations is accentuated by our inability to date the bulk of Old English poetry very closely. Clearly the earlier it is dated the more acceptable a high degree of pagan connotation would be. Even then we would have to accept that early Old English poetry may have been influenced in its choice of words by Latin models. For instance, when a verb like *gestigan* is used of mounting the cross, a word which is found already in the Ruthwell Cross portion of *The Dream of the Rood* from the eighth century, we may assume it is a reflection of the Latin *ascendere* the word commonly used in appropriate liturgical passages. If this is so, it may be difficult to think of any traditional literary Germanic connotation surviving: all that would survive would be the connotations at a colloquial level which are not recoverable.

Because of the alliterative metre Anglo-Saxon poets used a number of different words to mean the same thing or invented various circumlocutions to express the same concept. The many words and phrases for 'man' are typical. Apart from the simplex forms like *man, beorn, eorl* and *wiga*, there are compounds like *flotman, garberend randwiga*, and phrases like *beorscealca sum*. If we assume that the restrictions imposed by the alliterative metre motivated the poet to choose a particular word of phrase, this would imply that the connotation of this word or that phrase was unimportant. For the poets there may have been no connotative difference between *wiga* and *beorscealca sum*. It is reasonable to suggest that the difference between these expressions is more metrical and rhetorical than connotative. In the same way in the Old English poem *The Phoenix* the bird is referred to by words like *leodfruma* ('prince') which occur otherwise in works of the Germanic heroic tradition, and the phoenix's environment is portrayed as one suitable for heroes because the words used are also found in heroic poetry. The reason behind this is that the bird is allegorized as the good men who follow Christ and so there is an equation of phoenix = man. But as Old English poems generally deal with heroic attitudes, there is in them the equation of man = hero. Therefore, the equation phoenix = man in *The Phoenix* is expressed through the equation of phoenix = hero. It was hardly possible for the poet to refer to mankind and hence to the phoenix in a non-heroic way because the vocabulary in Old English poetry is heroic.[1] This means that in Old English poetry heroic vocabulary is unmarked and the poet of *The Phoenix* simply took over what was inherent in the language without deliberately seeking out words with an heroic connotation. The connotative value of these words was small. They may have been accepted broadly as poetic and consequently they may have had associations of a certain level of style; but they were not evocative individually. The choice of words was restricted, and we would be unwise to read into this poet's choice of

83

words an intention to exploit the connotations of the heroic vocabulary.

In Old English poetry variation, in which a concept is repeated by using another word or phrase with roughly the same meaning and form, occurs frequently. In *The Phoenix* lines 398–9

>   þenden eces word,
> halges hleoþorcwide, healdan woldan
> (whilst they observed the commands of God, the dictates of the Saviour),

eces word is a variant of *halges hleoporcwide*. Both mean ultimately the same thing, although *ece* means 'the eternal (one)' and *halig* 'the holy (one)', and *word* means 'word, command' and *hleoporcwide* means essentially the same although its literal meaning is something like 'sound speech'. Does the use of this type of variation make the employment of connotation in Old English poetry less likely? The answer is in the affirmative, particularly as many of the words do not seem to be strongly distinguished in the first place. While it is possible to hold the opinion that Anglo-Saxon poets did intend to increase the evocative meanings of a concept by heaping up variants, a comparison with later poetry suggests that this was not their primary purpose. When Shakespeare used variants, as for example in *Macbeth*:

> Sleep that knits up the ravell'd sleave of care,
> The death of each day's life, sore labour's bath,
> Balm of hurt minds, great Nature's second course,
> Chief nourisher in Life's feast (II. ii. 37–40),

he introduced a new image with each phrase and created a cumulative effect of various meanings. The reference of each phrase and even its construction were so different that the description contains depth of meaning without uniformity of expression. In Old English there is a greater repetitiveness. Not only do *eces word* and *halges hleoporcwide* repeat each other in form, for each is composed of an adjective in the genitive followed by a noun, but also each echoes the meaning of the other almost exactly. There is no expansion of the frame of reference. The variation is a rhetorical device used to give weight to the expression rather than to create an expansion of the range of meaning or imagery.

It may be appropriate now to consider an individual word in detail. Because it could have pagan affiliations, *wyrd* is a suitable one.[2] Associated with *weorþan* 'to become', *wyrd* has cognates in many Germanic languages. The most important of these is Old

Norse *Urðr*, the name of a pagan goddess usually translated as 'Fate'. Consequently it is reasonable to suppose that the word *wyrd* existed in the pagan Old English period in the sense 'fate', though it does not necessarily follow that the Anglo-Saxons had a goddess of that name. Because of the difficulty of dating the poetry it is better to start with the prose texts. For this word the principal prose source is Alfred's translation of Boethius' *De consolatione philosophiae* from the end of the ninth century. In this translation *wyrd* normally corresponds to Latin *fortuna* and means 'providence, lot, course of events', though 'fate' might be a possible translation in some passages. There is no sense of a personified fate; and the Latin *Parcae* are not translated by *Wyrda*: in contexts where *Parcae* occurs the Latin word is taken over directly into the Anglo-Saxon text. In Alfred's translation *wyrd* is a force subject to God's will and in many cases it represents his forethought. Other prose texts have the same range of reference. With poetry difficulties arise because we have no extant source to use as a basis for understanding what the Old English means. The range of possibilities lies between two poles. On the one hand, the parallel of the Old Norse *Urðr* suggests that *wyrd* was a pagan goddess who controlled men's destinies. There are many passages which might support this interpretation, such as *Wyrd bið ful aræd* ('Fate is absolutely inexorable' *The Wanderer* 5) and *hie wyrd forsweop on Grendles gryre* ('Fate swept them into Grendel's power' *Beowulf* 477–8). On the other hand, the examples in the Old English Boethius suggest that *wyrd* never was a goddess, but was simply a word used to express what befell man in his mortal existence. Other examples, or even those just quoted, could support this interpretation. The two meanings are not mutually exclusive, since one could have shaded easily into the other and both could have been operative among different people at one and the same time.

As we saw in the previous chapter modern editors are presented with a choice which did not face medieval readers because they have to decide whether to provide *wyrd* with an initial capital or not. Furthermore, this decision may breed a feeling in us that what a word means in one text is its meaning in all the other contemporary texts in which it occurs. It is quite possible, though, that some Old English readers thought of *wyrd* as a goddess and others as providence or man's lot. Ultimately we must admit ignorance of what the connotations of this word were in Old English poetry. We are left in the somewhat unhappy position that our subjective interpretation of a poem will influence our understanding of the meaning of important words in that poem. That we can prove a Christian philosophic sense for the word need not imply that a pagan sense is automatically excluded. It is almost always possible to point to a Christian connection for a word in at least some of its occurrences in Old English, though it is dangerous to assume it was the only or even the most dominant one in the period. Similarly words which to us might appear to have some mythological or pagan significance, like *wæl-ceosega* 'the chooser of the slain', may have existed in a neutral sense.[3] For this word is used to describe a raven, and any connection with the Valkyries may be purely fortuitous. The meaning of isolated words in medieval poems is likely to be so controversial that we have to interpret them from the poem rather than the poems from them.

Another type of word which might have significant native connotation is the runeword, for runes had connections with magic and religion. Each rune represents a letter of the alphabet, but it also has its own name like the Greek letters *alpha, beta,* etc. These names are common words like *eðel* 'native land', and it is possible that such words had more than usual significance for the Anglo-Saxons. The symbol sometimes replaces the word in some manuscripts, as in *Beowulf*:

> folc gehealdan
> hord ond hleoburh, hæleþa rice,
> *eðel* Scyldinga (911–13)
> (hold sway over the people, the treasure and citadel, the kingdom of warriors, the native land of the Scyldings),

where I have replaced the rune sign by its name in italics. But *eðel* neither demands nor deserves any emphasis here, and the rune sign is a scribal convenience with no indication of poetic connotation. The same is true of the use of runes by Cynewulf at the end of his poems to mark his signature. In these signatures the use of the runewords is twofold. The individual runes in their capacity as letters together form an acrostic on his name, whereas the meaning of the rune names fits in with the sense of the passage, even though it is somewhat forced. The runes are used to make the constituent parts of the acrostic stand out, for otherwise the average reader would have failed to notice the signature or a scribe might have altered some of the words to make better sense. Hence the runes carry no connotations; their use is antiquarian and punning rather than poetic. However, if in cases involving runes and the vocabulary of the heroic tradition it is impossible for us to trace any connotations with confidence, it is unlikely that we will be in a position to do so for native words of any other kind. This need not mean that Anglo-Saxon words were without connotations, but simply that we are unable to discover them. Nevertheless, the method of composition and the fragmentary nature of the poetic tradition do suggest that if words had connotations they were much weaker than the ones to which we are accustomed. We have to recognize also that the pleasure they gained from poetry came more from the rhetorical arrangement of words into pleasing patterns than from lexical evocation.

FOREIGN CONNOTATION

The difficulty of recognizing any indigenous connotations for Old English words has led many to assume that only medieval words which are associated with the equivalent word in a foreign language have connotations; these would naturally be learned connotations. These words are for the Old English period of Latin origin (or they are English translations of Latin words like *welwillendnes* from *benevolentia*) and for the Middle English period principally of French origin (though Latin is still an important source). Consequently recent scholarship is full of the assimilation of patristic ideas into Old English poetry, usually through the assumption that Old English words which occur only a few times have the same connotations which were attached to equivalent Latin words over centuries of exegesis and comment. Hence Old English poetry is given a very Christian colouring to the exclusion of possible pagan or Germanic implications. A typical example is the word *ofermod* in *The Battle of Maldon*. The two interrelated stages in interpreting this word are firstly that it means 'pride', and secondly that in this meaning it carries with it all the moral connotations of *superbia*, the equivalent word in Latin.

The way to understand the meaning of a compound like *ofermod* might be as follows: to see in what other contexts the word occurs, to see how the two parts of the compound are used either as simplex words or in other compounds, to consider the meaning of other words which fall in the same semantic field, and to consider those words which are its antonyms, having an opposite meaning. It is often assumed, without much justification, that the first method is the most important. For if the composition of Old English poetry was fragmented, we have to recognize that both author and audience might have been ignorant of the other examples in the literature. We can more readily adduce parallels than they could. The meanings of words were much more fluid than we allow. In this particular case we need to remember that *The Battle of Maldon* may have been composed as late as 1030.[4] If so, it would have arisen after the Scandinavian conquest of England by Canute, and this might explain why there were so many Scandinavian influences in it. In this case lexical parallels for *ofermod* might have to be sought in Scandinavian rather than in Old English poetry, a feature which reinforces the concept of the fragmented nature of Old English poetic composition. While it is possible that *ofermod* in *The Battle of Maldon* means 'pride', it is essential to recognize that its semantic field of reference includes such concepts as bravery, excess, high spirits and heroism. This range of meaning is implied by the simplex *mod* and by related words such as *wlenco* which can be used of either heroism or pride. Even if we could assume that the compound *ofermod* was formed as a translation of the Latin *superbia*, the semantic field of the two words could never be identical because of the inherited meaning of the two parts of the Old English compound, of the difference in social background and attitudes of the users of each literature, and of the different contexts in which the words occur. *Ofermod*, for example, never occurs in those contexts where *superbia* is most distinctively used in Latin, in lists of the seven deadly sins. It is used in poems of conflict like *The Battle of Maldon* which deal with heroism and heroic postures, in which the moral behaviour of the action described is susceptible to different interpretations. An English audience would react to a man's *ofermod* in a battle poem in quite a different way from his understanding of *superbia* in stories of biblical or classical characters. The Bible after all was used in teaching, and the moral attitudes to adopt to the events described in it were clearly laid down by biblical commentators; differences of interpretation were to a large extent excluded. The background of the two words was so diverse that the ranges of meaning were quite distinct. That both today are often translated 'pride' merely obscures that essential difference.

Each word was used in a different way. The English language was in a state of rapid development as a result of which the vocabulary changed throughout the medieval period. This prevented any uniformity from being established in basic meaning, let alone in connotation. *Superbia* had fixed moral associations and would inevitably be used by writers of Latin works in certain contexts. *Ofermod*, however, was so infrequently used that it never became associated with a particular context. If an Anglo-Saxon came across the word *superbia* in a Latin text he was translating he might have rendered it by *ofermod*, but he could just as easily have used *wlenco* or one of the other words in existence, or he could have invented a new compound. A Middle English translator would have an equally large, but different, range of words from which to choose. It was only in the late Middle English period that *pride* became the most common word to translate *superbia*, though even then writers like Reginald Pecock still insisted on creating native English words rather than using foreign ones for concepts like this. Consequently it was only towards the end of the medieval period that an English word began to approximate in its literary connotations to the Latin *superbia*. Yet modern commentators give the impression that the connotations of a word like *superbia* can readily be detached from that word and can be grafted on to the equivalent word or words in medieval English. This is absurd, for languages do not work in that way. Each word in English like *ofermod* and *wlenco* has its own semantic field, which may have overlapped with that for *superbia*, but an exact equivalence is out of the question. The constant change in vocabulary, the variety of translators, and the absence of any one English text like the Bible to provide a model for uniformity of use prevented any such equivalence from being established in the medieval period. If this is true for a relatively common word in Christian Latin writing like *superbia*, which most educated Christians knew, how much more does it apply to less usual words in Latin. Yet many scholars proceed on the assumption that provided an Old English word can be equated with a Latin word, the former will bear all the associations and connotations of the latter. While we may accept that the concept of pride was well known to English readers, we must guard against the temptation to extend all the connotations of a word like *superbia* to all its possible English equivalents.

One might suppose that this inability to transfer connotative meaning from one language to another applied more to Old than to Middle English in that the early vocabulary was a native one in which the number of loanwords is limited. In Middle English, however, words were borrowed directly from French in their French form; and as French was spoken by many Englishmen it is possible that the connotations associated with a word in French were taken over when the word was introduced into English. The French words which are of most importance in this respect are those associated with courtly love, for it is essential in reading Middle English poetry to know whether words like *danger* and *prisoner* bear the same associations of the courtly love ethos in English which they had in French. With these words the fact that French was spoken in England would seem to be immaterial since any connotations these words carried were literary ones which would almost certainly not be reflected at the colloquial level. These words acquired their significance by being grouped together in certain themes in courtly poetry.

While it is difficult to be certain, it is likely that the English words did not have the same connotations as their French counterparts. In the Middle English period we take Chaucer as our norm and assume that all authors and readers were as familiar with French literary works as he was. This can hardly have been the case. Many translations were made by hack writers who were ignorant of what had been translated in the past and were uncertain of the significance of the words they transferred bodily into English. For literary connotation to flourish there must be a closeknit group of writers and audience such as those found in the provincial French courts and such as was to exist in England at the royal court in the late sixteenth century. Although the court of Richard II had the makings of such a tight group, it did not survive long enough to produce any lasting effect in lexical usage. Furthermore, a key text in the French courtly tradition like the *Roman de la Rose* was not translated into English till the late fourteenth century so that part of the essential literary background to understanding the courtly tradition and the connotations of some of its words was missing. No doubt many English readers and translators were aware that certain words of French origin were expected in certain scenes, but it is difficult to escape the conclusion that they were unfamiliar with the significance these words had in French. For many Englishmen such words amounted to little more than a convention or game, whose only significance was that they occurred in such passages. The words gave the right tone to the passage in question, but did not bring any further connotations. We can see in their use a desire to elevate style and imitate such sophistication, but no attempt to exploit lexical suggestiveness. For example, the English translator of *Partonope of Blois* says at lines 2347-9 that he cannot understand the 'sentiment' of his French author:

> He tellyth hys tale of sentament,
> I vnder-stonde noȝth hys entent,
> Ne wolle ne besy me to lere.[5]

He used the words, but he did not appreciate their full significance.

Some of the better authors may have used some of these words more meaningfully, as perhaps the author of *Sir Gawain and the Green Knight* did at lines 1208 ff, where the lady treats Gawain in his bed as her 'prisoner', which is the major image of the stanza. If this is so, we have to accept that the words were much looser and weaker in their associations and connotations than the corresponding French words and that the majority of readers and listeners were not aware of the associations the poet was drawing upon. By and large it is better to assume that most words of the courtly love tradition were treated by English writers and readers as conventional, without any of the reverberations of meaning found in the equivalent French one; they simply lacked life.

THE POWER AND STYLISTIC LEVEL OF INDIVIDUAL WORDS

This chapter so far prompts the question whether medieval writer or audience thought that some words had more force than others and belonged to different stylistic levels. Undoubtedly they did recognize that words belonged to different styles, though it is sometimes difficult for us today to decide how to judge their response to the words. This applies particularly to French words in the Middle English period which may have been introduced into English at the spoken level before they entered the literary language. Because we can point to their origin, there is a natural tendency for us to regard all such words as learned. Hence they would be part of a high style. Thus Dr Brewer writes in reference to the openings of Chaucer's *General Prologue*:

> The passage is written in a modified 'high style'. The first two lines are simple and direct, so that no listener or reader can miss the point. The next three lines, with their almost scientifically elaborate mention of the nourishing of plants, are written in that poetic diction for which Chaucer was so venerated in the following two centuries; he calls water, *licour*, the West wind *Zephirus*.[6]

The implication is that *licour* was introduced to create a high style, as though it were a marked form as compared with the unmarked *water*. Is this so? It is not easy to be certain, but it is a common French word and it was used in other texts before Chaucer. In the English translation of Archbishop Thoresby's Latin *Catechism* made in 1357 we find:

> Another is, that it be done anely in water,
> For nanothir licour is leuefull tharfore.[7]

The passage deals with the seven sacraments and as far as we can tell it is not written in a high style; yet the translator uses *licour* as well as *water*. It may be that *licour* was a more common word than we allow, though it may have been included in this passage to increase the alliteration. As this translation was made in or near York, it appears that the word was well known in the north of England by the middle of the fourteenth century. This suggests that it would have been equally familiar by then in the south where French words were more common. What appears to us to be an elevated word because we know its origin may not have been so to Chaucer's audience who could have been ignorant of its origin. The passage's style may in fact be indicated more by the syntax Chaucer used than by the choice of words.

Modern usage may be an indifferent guide to the stylistic levels of medieval words. Caxton, for instance, made a translation of the French *Fierabras* which he published as *Charles the Great* in 1483. The French text uses *face* and *visaige* indiscriminately, but Caxton rendered both words *visage*. It is possible to interpret Caxton's choice as an attempt to elevate the language by choosing a less common word, though a study of his translating habits indicates that this is not the correct interpretation.[8] The more satisfactory conclusion is that for Caxton's time *visage* was a more common word than *face*. This example implies that there are many words in medieval English which we evaluate stylistically on the basis of the status of their modern equivalents. Since the vocabulary of the medieval period has not been studied in depth, it is not possible to tell whether such assumptions are correct or not.

Many medieval writers certainly thought that English words lacked much power or significance, particularly in relation to Latin and French words. Authors frequently introduced Latin and French words into their works, and when they did so it was because the English equivalents did not have sufficient associations. Thus the Parson in *The Canterbury Tales* says: 'and bireveth hire thilke precious fruyt that the book clepeth the hundred fruyt. I ne kan seye it noon ootherweyes in Englissh, but in Latyn it highte *Centesimus fructus*' (x 868). Here there can be little doubt that the Parson felt the English expression unsatisfactory because it lacked the connotations which the Latin phrase had. The English words had not been subjected to frequent comment and elucidation by scholars and so lacked any associations. To the Parson the English was flat and almost meaningless. This inadequacy of English as a means of learned exposition was commented on by Langland in *Piers Plowman* B XIV 277–8:

> 'I kan noȝt construe', quod haukyn; 'ye moste kenne me þis
> on englissh.'
> 'Al þis in englissh', quod Pacience, 'it is wel hard to
> expounen.'

Although it was surely quite possible to carry on a theological discussion in fourteenth-century English, many felt it an unsuitable language for such discussions because English words were felt to be inappropriate. The words could not carry the semantic load needed in commentaries of the kind Patience was thinking of; or so it seemed to writers like Langland who had in mind the example of

Latin with its richer and more clearly differentiated vocabulary. It may indeed be for this sort of reason that the author of *Sir Gawain and the Green Knight* used *pentangle* as well as its English equivalent *the endless knot*:

> Then þay schewed hym þe schelde, þat was of schyr goulez
> Wyth þe pentangel depaynt of pure gold hwez.
> . . . . and Englych hit callen
> Oueral, as I here, þe endeles knot. (619–30)

The poet may well have found the technical French word altogether more suggestive than its English counterpart. At the same time the inclusion of the English phrase may indicate that he was uncertain that his audience would have found the French as significant as he did. The same may apply to the Parson in the first example in this paragraph. Latin and French words were not more meaningful to the average audience in England, even if they were to those with a considerable familiarity with those languages. In all such cases the writer has to direct his reader to the original language or to point out this contrast with English so that he will look for more meaning in the word than he would otherwise have done. Learned words may have carried significant connotation in English only when an author pointed to this extra meaning.

Latin in particular was known to be a language with powerful words because there was a history behind the language and words had an origin that expressed some of their essence. Etymology was a familiar tool in Latin which was used by the fathers and sermon writers. When Latin, and to a lesser extent French, words were translated into English, attempts were made to keep these etymologies because it was realized they were essential for the meaning and force of the work. While this may at times have been the result of laziness alone, it was appreciated that the equivalent English words had no history and so the etymology of the Latin word had to be given. Thus in the Middle English translation of *The Mirror of St Edmund* we can find a passage like the following:

> And Hym calles men Godd by This skill[reason], For þis worde *Deus*, þat es to say, Godd, commes of a worde of grewe [Greek] þat es called *theos*, and þat es als mekill [much] for to say als ane anely Godd.[9]

What a person without Latin made of this is uncertain, except that Latin and Greek clearly had depths of meaning which were quite out of the reach of English. English words had no past and hence no inner significance which could be detected through etymology.

Some English writers did attempt to give etymologies in English. At its most basic level, the result is often odd. When Adam says of Eve in the fifteenth-century *Chester Mystery Cycle*:

> Therfore shee shalbe called, iwisse,
> 'viragoo', nothinge amisse;
> for out of man taken shee is,
> and to man shee shall drawe,[10]

the etymology of *virago* depends on the Latin *vir* 'man'. Since the poet has used the English word *man* instead of the Latin *vir*, all those with no Latin would have been at sea although they may have known it was an etymology which was frequently cited. This example shows simply an attempt to make a Latin etymology into an English one. Other authors were more constructive in their approach. Langland in *Piers Plowman* B XV 459 wrote:

> Heþen is to mene after heeþ and vntiled erþe.

Here Langland suggests that *heathen* is derived from *heath*, though his inclusion of *and vntiled erþe* shows that he did not have etymology only or even principally in mind. This etymology may in fact be correct, though it seems likely that Langland made the assumption on the similarity of the two English words assisted by the parallel of Latin *paganus*. For *paganus* meant both 'pagan' and 'rustic', as the ancient idolatry survived longest in the late Roman Empire among isolated villagers and peasants. Since this dual meaning of *paganus* would be familiar to Latinate Englishmen like Langland, it is easy to see how he guessed that *heathen* meant 'the heathdwellers' and was consequently related to *heath*. It is difficult to exclude the influence of Latin here.

A purely native example is provided by Chaucer in his *Legend of Good Women* F 182–5:

> But for to loke upon the dayesie,
> That wel by reson men it calle may
> The "dayesye," or elles the "ye of day,"
> The emperice and flour of floures alle.

This perhaps hardly merits the description of etymology, for all Chaucer did was to take the parts of a compound and reverse their order. In some ways this is more like revitalizing a tired word than etymology. However, that Chaucer introduced it does show that etymology was a powerful force and that many writers realized how poor English was in this connection as compared with Latin. The example may lack sophistication, but it does indicate a felt need in the language. It is also significant that many of these examples come from the later Middle English period for that was a time when the insufficiency of English was most keenly felt. Chaucer's example shows how easy it was to break up compounds in order to give an appearance of inner strength in the word. This system could have been exploited by the Anglo-Saxon poets, since their poetry is replete with compounds, but it never was. Even many of the calques formed on the basis of Latin words, like *welwillendnes* from *benevolentia*, were not given the etymological treatment. It was only as men became more conscious of the poverty of English in relation to other languages that they tried to rectify the position.

HARD WORDS AND POETIC WORDS

It is natural to enquire whether there were any 'hard' words or 'poetic' words in medieval literature, for in both cases it might appear that the writer had gone to some trouble to find an unusual word which he expected his audience to respond to in a particular way. What happened when a medieval reader came across a word he did not understand or whose meaning he only dimly grasped because it was a new creation or a loanword? We must remember how rarely we read a text, whether medieval or modern, which is not to some extent prepared and smoothed for us. The text may have notes and glossary; and if not, there are dictionaries and critical works which we can readily consult. When such aids are not available, as is true for some very modern literature, we may easily dismiss what we find unintelligible as not worth the effort of further study or reading. There were many words and phrases which were unintelligible in medieval texts, as the evidence of scribal copying reveals only too clearly.

The general effect of scribal intervention was to reduce the vocabulary to the lowest common denominator: unusual words and names were replaced. To many writers some words no doubt were of uncertain meaning and they may have been included because they sounded right or were in the source used. Thus in his *Reynard the Fox*, Caxton translated a list of animal names from his Dutch prose original as follows: 'Tho cam forth many a beest anon, as the squyrel, the musehont, the fychews, the martron, the beuer wyth his wyf ordegale, the genete, the ostrole, the bonssyng, and the fyret.'[11] It is more than probable that Caxton himself did not know exactly what some of these words meant (if they can be said to have any meaning at all). The word *ostrole*, for example, was taken over directly from his source, which in its turn took it from the Flemish poetic version which was its source. The ultimate origin of this word was French, though as it occurs only in these examples in English and Dutch, one may question whether it really had any meaning in these languages. Caxton presumably understood it as some kind of animal, and this is how his readers would understand it as well. They are not likely to have known what animal it was, and perhaps its exact meaning was immaterial to them in that the name occurs in a list of animals which play no part in the story.

Although this example is taken from a relatively minor text from a literary point of view, I have chosen it because many may more readily agree to the proposition in a minor text. But it is a situation which occurs frequently in medieval literature, whether minor or major, for where elevation of vocabulary is prized words are often chosen more for their sound than for their meaning. The names in the list of medical authors found in the description of the physician in *The General Prologue* (*The Canterbury Tales* I. 429–34) are likely to have been as unfamiliar to most readers as Caxton's animals. Certainly medieval scribes found difficulty in copying them. Today, however, a writer will direct his work at a particular market and seek to explain the terms that he thinks would be unclear or unfamiliar to that audience. Such specialization was unknown in the medieval period, and because of the fragmented nature of the literary tradition an inability to understand all the words in a piece of writing must have been an everyday experience. The large amount of translation, much of it fairly literal, would inevitably lead to the large influx of foreign words into English; even Chaucer is credited with the introduction of many loanwords from French. The resulting problem of intelligibility was one that in the sixteenth century was to concern Richard Mulcaster in *The First Part of the Elementarie* (1581) but it was just as pressing earlier. In the sixteenth century dictionaries of hard words and glossaries were compiled to help readers, but no such aids existed in the medieval period. Readers with only a small smattering of French or Latin would necessarily understand the general drift of a text without worrying too much about individual words. Indeed, this is not an uncommon phenomenon among ordinary readers today. In the medieval period this tendency may have been accentuated by the inheritance of the oral tradition in that words were most meaningful when they were part of set phrases or themes.[12] And the generalizing trend in medieval literature would in any case make words less particular than they are today. Since both heroic and chivalric literature were concerned with ideals, it would not be reasonable to expect that they looked for distinguishing personal characteristics among exponents of similar ideals.

The tendency towards the general and the grouping of the same words within traditional themes are important reasons for the absence of a poetic vocabulary in medieval English. There were few striking nouns or adjectives which drew attention to themselves by being unusual or different; on the contrary, the vocabulary was traditional and (to modern taste) overburdened with clichés. Compounds in Old English were formed on familiar patterns and had none of that sensuous or picturesque quality associated with compounds in Shakespeare and Keats. Even such apparently colourful ones as *urigfeþra* 'dewy feathered' (*The Seafarer* 25) turn out to be traditional in construction and use. There is no evidence here of straining after poetic effect. In Middle English the borrowing of French words was for the broadening of English style; it was not for the increase of the poetic quality or subtlety of the vocabulary. Even Chaucer who is praised from the fifteenth century onwards for his command of language used only one phrase which we would regard as hauntingly evocative, the 'smoky reyn' of *Troilus and Criseyde* III 628. It was for this reason that C. S. Lewis rejected the reading of the Auchinleck manuscript of *Sir Orfeo* line 285 'Wiþ dim cri & bloweing'. In his opinion the line was too poetic, and hence not likely to be original.[13] The *dim* is probably a misreading for *dun*, a dialect variant of *din*, so that the line should read 'Wiþ din, cri & bloweing', as suggested by a reading in another manuscript. The use of words with roughly the same meaning is much more common in medieval literature than the use of evocative and individual adjectives. Individual words were interpreted in a general way through their surroundings: *ostrole* is an animal name because it occurs in a list of animal names, and *din* is a variant of *cri* and *bloweing*. Words were chosen to blend in with their surroundings and not to call attention to themselves by their meaning or other unusual qualities. They were more in the nature of rhetorical than semantic counters.

REPETITION

It is because words had less particular meaning in the medieval period that various forms of repetition are found in works written at that time. The most common types are the use of doublets in which one word is joined by *and* to a synonym or closely related word, variation by which a phrase or clause is repeated with different words but with a similar rhythm, and straightforward repetition of the same word. The last of these strikes a modern reader forcefully since it is common nowadays never to repeat a word; it is one of the few stylistic prejudices which most of us carry away from our schooling. To the medieval writer repetition was an essential method of preventing misunderstanding, of making sure that what you wanted to say was emphasized, and of forestalling the corruption of meaning through scribal mistakes or corrections. At its most blatant it might take this form adopted by Chaucer in the Pardoner's prologue to his tale:

> And over al this, avyseth yow right wel
> What was comaunded unto Lamuel –
> Nat Samuel, but Lamuel, seye I. (VI. 583–5)[14]

One can imagine that without this last line many scribes would have changed Lamuel to Samuel because he was the better known figure in the Bible. Indeed, the last line could almost be understood as a direct address to Adam, Chaucer's scribe; it shows how conscious Chaucer was of corruption. It also indicates one solution an author adopted to protect himself against its unfortunate results.

More typical of medieval repetition are the passages in which a word is repeated frequently, as in this scene from *Piers Plowman* B III 219–24:

> Beggeres for hir biddynge bidden of men Mede;
> Mynstrales for hir myrþe Mede þei aske;
> The kynge haþ mede of his men to make pees in londe;
> Men þat kenne clerkes crauen of hem Mede;
> Preestes þat prechen þe peple to goode
> Asken Mede and massepens and hire mete als.

This type of repetition was designed to create emphasis rather than to prevent corruption, though undoubtedly it would have helped in that respect too. Today the use of different type faces and the relative absence of printing mistakes allow authors to use a wide variety of means to achieve their emphases, some of which can be fairly subtle. As a medieval author was unable to prevent changes by scribes to his work he had to create his emphases more deliberately by pointing to them by repetition and other means. At first this procedure may strike us as laboured and crude. This is particularly the case with didactic literature in which it is essential that key words should be defined and stressed. Often works of didactic literature are little more than extended commentaries on such words. Because this type of writing is out of favour now, there is a tendency to dismiss their typical stylistic features, such as repetition, as naive or simple. But the repetition of key words, such as *gentillesse* in *The*

Franklin's Tale, is found in more sophisticated texts. The reason is the same in both types of literature: to point to what is significant.

Doublets and variation were used throughout the medieval period and indeed long afterwards. In the sixteenth century a teacher like Mulcaster could try to turn doublets to educational use by recommending that of the two words one might be native and the other foreign so that less educated people could become familiar with the foreign terms which were being adopted wholesale into the language. To writers in the Old and Middle English periods, however, doublets were a stylistic device used to create verbosity or various rhythmical effects, and their frequent use suggests that the meaning of a word was less important than its sound and its ability to be paired, for there can be no doubt that the constant use of doublets *does* weaken the significance inherent in the individual parts. Whereas *onde* might be used to mean 'envy', it was so frequently used in the doublet *niþ and onde* that the word by itself appears to lack weight or significance. Words kept a certain company and were most meaningful within that company. In addition, variation may create the same weakening of meaning, for the elements which make up the variation tend to be repetitive rather than cumulative. Medieval rhetoricians recommended the use of phrasal and clausal balance and this in its turn would encourage variation, in which the harmony of sound was more valued than the extension of meaning. Some types of composition, like the alliterative halfline, fall naturally into phrasal patterns whose rhythmic similarity encourages repetition so that it is hardly surprising that similar phrases recur in alliterative works.

The theme of this rather discursive chapter has been that words in medieval English lacked the same clear-cut significance or connotative associations of modern words. With the rise of a standard language, words outside the standard will automatically develop connotation by the very virtue of that fact, and this process will speed up an interest in individual words and their differences. This was not a situation that had been reached in the medieval period. English writers at that time were well aware of the power of words, but felt that English lacked the necessary ingredients to enable words to be used evocatively. A language like Latin had a history and had been used for the composition of literature for many centuries; there was an accepted and known tradition in both language and literature. Although by the end of the medieval period literature had been written in English for hundreds of years, knowledge of the previous literature and language was to all intents and purposes non-existent. English appeared to be a language without a past and with a literature that was always modern. Hence words could not attract to themselves those associations linked with known literary works or linguistic origins. English words were insubstantial things which had to be given meaning by various devices such as repetition. The overall effect of this lack of lexical strength was that the literature was more concerned with moral values and narrative effects than with linguistic subtleties. For us this presents a problem of interpretation since we set great store by close linguistic criticism. We are always in danger of loading onto a medieval English word far more significance than it was meant to carry. Our eagerness to do so can lead to a misunderstanding of such features as word-play, parody and themes. These three topics will form the subjects of the following chapters.

5

Word-Play

As different kinds of word-play have come to play an increasing
part in criticism of modern literature, the influence of this development has been felt within the study of medieval literature. It is rare
nowadays to pick up a critical work dealing with medieval literature
which does not involve a consideration of ambiguity, punning, satire
or irony. Indeed, 'puns' are recorded incidentally in pieces of criticism
which deal with quite different concerns, as though it is natural to
find puns at every turn and to record them.[1] Yet no study has
sought to tackle the problem more generally by investigating how
relevant these features are for an understanding of medieval English
literature or in what ways they were used (if at all) by authors at
the time.

Typical of modern criticism is a recent book on Old English poetry
by J. H. Wilson called *Christian Theology and Old English Poetry*.
I would like to consider what the premises of this book are without
seeking to imply by my choice of it that it is better or worse than
many similar books. In his exposition of the Old English *Exodus* Mr
Wilson finds a pun to almost every twenty-five lines of Old English
poetry, the first of which is appropriately enough in the opening
lines: 'The word play in the opening lines is equally important, since
it sets the tone and theme at the outset. In the opening three lines

> Hwæt! We feor and neah   gefrigen hábað
> ofer middangeard   Moyses domas,
> wræclico wordriht,   wera cneorissum, –

> 'Lo! We far and near have learned
> throughout the world the laws of Moses,
> wondrous law to the generations of men, –'

there is a pun on the word *wræclico*. Literally the word may be
translated 'wondrous', but it also means 'wretched, miserable', and

is related to the noun *wrecca* or *wræcca* meaning 'exile, wanderer, pilgrim'. 'The pun gives added meaning to the lines by suggesting that the theme of the poem will have to do not only with the Laws of Moses but also with man's exile, as that exile is related to the convenant between God and man.'[2] Here the absence of any discussion of the language is what is most striking. The adjective *wræclico* is said to be 'related' (whatever that might imply) to the noun *wrecca* or *wræcca*, and it is therefore assumed that the adjective also implies any senses associated with the noun. This is simply asserted, not argued. There is no discussion of either noun or adjective to discover whether the contexts in which they occur are such that it is reasonable to accept that one might also evoke the other. There is no attempt to consider whether *wrecca* or *wræcca* is the commoner form of the noun, for if it is the former the difference in vowel sounds between *wræclico* and *wrecca* may have prevented any association between the words from developing. Finally, there is no clue left by the Old English author in this sentence to help the reader or listener appreciate that he might understand *wræclico* in any sense other than its expected one. There are other assumptions in this 'pun', but all that need be said now is that if we accept that any word can carry with it the senses of any of its 'related' words then every word in Anglo-Saxon may embrace a score of puns – a feature of their language which the Anglo-Saxons may well have found tiresome.

Naturally verbal manipulation was known and practised in medieval England, but that does not mean that words were manipulated in the ways to which we have become accustomed today. It is necessary to elaborate some of the points made in my second chapter. The absence of a standard language led to the composition of literary works in a variety of dialects. When these works were copied the language was often altered to make it suitable for a different dialect or for the linguistic conditions prevailing at a later date. Either development could influence those puns which were based on two words of different meaning which happened to have the same pronunciation. For example, H. Kökeritz claims that in *Twelfth Night* Fabian's 'if I loose a scruple of this sport, let me be boyl'd to death with Melancholly' (II. v. 2–4) is based on a pun of *boil* and *bile* which were pronounced sufficiently alike at that time to be accepted as homophones.[3] I will refer to this type of pun as a 'concealed pun', because only one word is given in the literary text and the other has to be inferred by listener or reader from the homophonic nature of the words. The two words forming the pun in *Twelfth Night* are no longer homophones, and it may be that even in Shakespeare's time not every speaker pronounced them alike. Consequently the difficulties a writer faced in using the concealed pun are that it is unstable, in that the pronunciation may change, and local in that the identity of pronunciation may not be found among all speakers of the language.

These difficulties apply to some extent to rhymes as well as to puns, but with the former a reader is at least presented with two words which he knows are supposed to have the same sound even if they do not in his own speech. In *The General Prologue* at lines 3–4 no modern reader is deceived by the current pronunciation to claim that Chaucer did not intend *licour* to rhyme with *flour*. The rhyming scheme in Chaucer is clear to all; and each makes the best of it he can. But few modern readers would suspect that there is a pun on *boyl'd* in *Twelfth Night* unless they were informed of this fact by the notes of their edition, for there is no indication from the arrangement of the words that there is any significant sound-effect there. The only clues are the nature of the verbal exchange and the characters of the speakers. In order to understand the difficulty that scribes found themselves in we have only to reflect on our own ignorance in the case of this pun. If a scribe in the medieval period spoke in a different dialect from, or lived at a later date than the author whose text he was copying, there would be many puns which he would not understand and so would fail to preserve as he modernized the language or altered the dialect. The problems facing scribes were known to authors, as Chaucer's words to Adam imply, and this knowledge would act as a constraint upon them. It is not that punning was necessarily any less possible then than now (though the more inflections a language has, the less easy punning is), but simply that the conditions of the language and of the reproduction of literature would discourage certain types of punning in literary works, perhaps in particular that of the concealed pun where the matching homophone is only implied from the passage.

We may also remember that there was no standardized spelling in medieval England although there were various local attempts to achieve some uniformity. Most manuscripts exhibit a wide range of spellings within themselves, let alone when contrasted with other manuscripts from the same time. This absence of standardization would prevent playing with the spelling of words to achieve a punning effect as is found in later periods. John Keats, for example, in a letter to George and Georgina Keats could write: 'Nothing strikes me so forcibly with a sense of the rediculous as love . . . His pathetic visage becomes irrisistable',[4] in which he spells ridiculous *rediculous* (to imply the red of blushing) and irresistible *irrisistable* (to imply an inability to resist risibility). This kind of word-play demands a uniform orthography and was not feasible in medieval England when the appropriate conditions did not exist. Even in Shakespeare's time

orthography was sufficiently unsettled for Kökeritz to claim that 'no
Shakespearean pun was ever based upon the spelling of a word;
either meaning or pronunciation is involved, but never orthography.'[5] He thus rejects many of the suggested word-plays discovered by critics working from written texts.

The effect that this linguistic situation had on the medieval writer
is easy to appreciate. He would have to arrange his material carefully so that the word-play was clearly marked out. This would
enable both reader and scribe to react in the desired way. The concealed pun would be difficult to preserve in a medieval English text
and so is less likely to be found, though this need not mean that it
was never introduced by any writers. It is usually difficult, however,
to be certain that such puns were intentional. The modern search
for subtlety in literature has led to the discovery of a large number
of concealed puns in medieval literary works; it seems likely that
few of these were intended by their authors. We saw, for example, in
chapter three how Chaucer had to labour the point that he was
referring to a title of a book because scribes did not in general use a
different script to signify titles. If he was forced to be so explicit in
what to us is such a simple thing as a book title, how much less
likely is it that he would introduce concealed puns which many
readers would simply not understand were there? These poems which
have a first-person narrator can use him to prepare the audience for
the word-play or irony, though this more prosaic role of the narrator
is often overlooked. Thus in the description of the Monk in *The
General Prologue* Chaucer adds the line: 'And I seyde his opinion was
good' (I. 183). We today may feel that this comment is superfluous
since we are quite used to catching the ironies inherent in such
descriptions as that of the Monk. But Chaucer's line directs the
contemporary audience's attention firmly to the Monk's views of his
profession and emphasizes the word *good* which receives further stress
from its position as a rhyme word. Hence he is able to imply that
good may have more than its surface meaning and that the Monk's
opinion of his professional life may not be the best one. This line is
marked in Middle English literature because it is unusual to have
expressions of personal authority in moral or religious matters. We
expect moral or religious opinions to be confirmed by recourse to
accepted practice (i.e. proverb) or approved authorities (i.e. the
fathers). That a monk's views should be confirmed as good by a lay
narrator is strikingly different from what a medieval reader was used
to, and we may assume that this would lead him to reflect on the
nature of the views expressed. In addition, the line is rhetorically
contrived; it has been suggested that it is an example of the figure
antiphrasis, a rhetorical figure in which words are used in a sense

opposite to their proper meaning.[6] By the use of such markers Chaucer is able to imply that some words are more significant than they appear; but equally without such clear signposts those words might be passed over by scribe and contemporary reader as unexceptionable. We should remember the usefulness of the narrator in helping to point out irony and word-play; it may be that the greater use of the narrator in the fourteenth century was one reason why the poetry of that age had far more word-play than that of the Anglo-Saxon period. The narrator presents the reader with a different point of view within the poem in question and so naturally tends to create a tension between the ideals of the characters and those of the narrator, a situation which lends itself to certain kinds of ambiguity.

There were naturally other ways of directing attention to a particular word. Metrical features could be exploited, as indeed happened frequently in Middle English lyrics. In the previous paragraph we saw how *good* was accentuated by the rhyme, and this type of emphasis could be brought about through alliteration or stanza or metrical stress. When the poet of *Judith* wrote: 'hloh ond hlydde, hlynede ond dynede' (23), he exploited the fact that the Old English poetic halfline consisted of two stresses which naturally throw the two stressed words in the halfline into a close relationship. The poet could develop that relationship by introducing rhyme to accentuate it in what was otherwise an alliterative poem. He was thus able to create a word-play on *hlynede ond dynede* which contrasted with the alliteration on *hl-* in the rest of the line.

In the same way an author could use rhetorical conventions to draw attention to his word-play, as Chaucer did *antiphrasis*. Indeed some rhetorical figures of speech involved word-play, as did a figure like *oxymoron*, which is still used. It was always possible for an author to use the special resources of the language to draw attention to his word-play. Cynewulf in the Anglo-Saxon period used the runic symbols in his acrostic signature to indicate that there was an acrostic present – as we noted in the last chapter. Similarly in that chapter we saw that some Latin words were known to have an etymology. It was possible for an author to exploit this etymology to draw attention to a word and so indulge in word-play. Langland in his 'That Cardinals ben called and closynge yates' (B Prol. 104) used the etymology of *cardinal* from *cardo* 'a hinge'. Although the author was here using the etymology of the word, the way in which the line was constructed with its *ben called* helps to draw attention to the relationship between *Cardinals* and *closynge yates*. The poet has made it clear to the reader that he should look further into the words of this line. These then were some of the ways medieval authors indicated that word-play was present.

TYPES OF WORD-PLAY

Up till now in this chapter I have used both 'pun' and 'word-play' without defining them. It is time to attempt a categorization of the different types of word-play, for the recognition that some types are found in medieval English literature has led many to assume that all types are. One of the major shortcomings of criticism of medieval literature so far has been the absence of discrimination in dealing with word-play, for articles devoted to this subject have tended to gather in examples of many different kinds without distinguishing them.[7]

The most elementary kind is playing with the letters of a word to create a puzzle or acrostic. As we have already seen this type of word-play was unusual in medieval English because the spelling of words was not sufficiently stable to permit it. It was, however, a type known to English authors from its occurrence in Latin writings and some traditional Latin examples were transferred to English. In the N-town plays from the fifteenth century we find:

> here þis name Eva is turnyd Aue
> þat is to say withowte sorwe ar ȝe now.[8]

Eva is the Latin form of Eve who by biting the apple in Paradise brought original sin into the world. *Ave*, which is *Eva* in reverse, is the first word of the Latin greeting by the Archangel Gabriel to the Virgin Mary announcing that she would conceive a son, Jesus. Thus the original sin introduced by Eve would be reversed, as the names imply, and man would be brought out of sorrow back to Paradise. This word-play is traditional and is found in the writings of many Latin fathers; its popularity in later medieval times probably arose through its occurrence in the Latin writings of St Bernard of Clairvaux. The use of runes by Cynewulf to form his signature may also be regarded as of this type. In the later Middle Ages Thomas Usk formed an acrostic rubric MARGARETE OF VIRTW HAVE MERCI ON THIN USK in his work *The Testament of Love* (*c.* 1386) by using the initial letter of each chapter. As chapters were often provided with large illuminated capitals, the capitals stood out and so formed ideal elements in an acrostic signature. However, corruption could easily cause the acrostic to be lost, as happened in this case, because chapters became transposed and were even introduced with different words. No one reading Thynne's edition of Usk in the sixteenth century, would have been in a position to unravel the acrostic because of this disturbance. A similar type of acrostic is found in Thomas Norton's *Ordinal of Alchemy* (*c.* 1477).[9] Apart from these three, few English authors appear to have used acrostics to form their signatures, perhaps because signed works in English were relatively uncommon. Modern attempts to discover acrostics in other Middle English works, such as the *Ancrene Wisse* and the posited writings of Sir Richard Roos, do not seem to me to be successful, partly because they are too complicated.[10] They demand a stability in the text which is not found; there is nothing in these texts to encourage scribes to copy the important passages accurately.

One might expect riddles to fall into this category, but in their English examples they rarely involved word-play as such. They relied on abstruse knowledge or on the creation of an image with an element of the grotesque or misleading. The choice of individual words in the riddle is not significant and it is often as powerful in translation as in the original, as the following example translated from Old English shows:

> A creature came where many men, wise in mind, were sitting in the meeting-place; it had one eye and two ears and two feet, twelve hundred heads, back and belly, and two hands, arms, and shoulders, one neck and two sides. Say what is my name.[11]

The answer normally given is a One-eyed seller of garlic or onions. The incongruity of the description is as clear in Modern English as it was in Old English. In the same way it hardly seems appropriate to include number symbolism in this type of word-play for most attempts to explain medieval poems in this way include little that could be classified as word-play. Some scholars have suggested that we interpret the name *Octovyen* in Chaucer's *The Book of the Duchess* as a pun on 'eight (Christ) coming' [cf. Latin *octo* 'eight' and *via* 'way']; but this is not so much a pun as a symbolic shorthand of the poem's meaning according to this interpretation.[12] Where a poet has used some numerical formula to construct his poem, as may be the case with *Pearl*, this may throw certain lines into a relationship because they come at significant numerical sequences which may in turn put the words in those lines into some kind of play relationship. But it seems that this happens only with lines which conclude one stanza and open the next, or which are found at the beginning and end of the poem; and most of these examples are better dealt with under repetition than here.

The next type of word-play is what is now usually referred to as a 'jingle'. It involves a play on the sounds of words without necessarily extending the meaning or significance of those words. It was very popular in the Middle Ages and later, as frequent examples in Shakespeare's works testify, but has fallen out of fashion more recently because we regard it as more sophisticated to indulge in word-play involving meaning. To us today jingles seem artificial and childish; we prefer what we consider to be the more intellectual forms of ambiguity. But plays on sounds have a respectable ancestry and were recommended by the many rhetorical treatises which are found in the medieval period.[13] Such treatises were in Latin and were intended to help composition in Latin, but their precepts for word-play could readily be transferred to the vernacular. Some authors like Richard Rolle who wrote in both English and Latin used such rhetorical flourishes in either language. Other authors like Chaucer may have applied the practice of the rhetoricians from studying their treatises, for he refers in *The Nun's Priest's Tale* (vii. 3347) to Geoffrey of Vinsauf who wrote a treatise of this sort, or by copying the word-play in the French works used as models, particularly the poems of Guillaume de Machaut and the *Roman de la Rose*. Certainly the vogue for translation from French which is found in England in the fourteenth and fifteenth centuries was partly inspired by the admiration for the French authors' use of rhetoric.

Unfortunately the terms used to describe the various kinds of word-play differ in the many rhetorical treatises that survive from the medieval and renaissance periods. It is not my intention nor is it germane to my purpose to provide a comprehensive list of the jingles recommended, but only to give some indication of their variety. Hence I shall not introduce any of the technical names here in the hope that this may avoid confusion. Rhyming effects and alliteration are the two types most commonly found. The opening of the prose treatise *The Wooing of Our Lord* from the early thirteenth century is an example of the pervasive influence of alliteration in the medieval period: 'Jesu, swete Jesu, mi druth, mi derling, mi drihtin, mi healend, mi huniter, mi haliwei, swetter is munegunge of the then mildeu o muthe.'[14] The repetition of the *d-*, *h-*, and *m-* sounds is insistent and to us rather laboured. Many traditional phrases like *weal and woe* and similes like *as red as a rose* are formed on an alliterative base. We have already noted how some later scribes felt Chaucer indulged in too much alliteration and made attempts to reduce it. By itself alliteration is a relatively simple sound effect. For greater sophistication it was possible to link alliteration with various kinds of consonance. In *Piers Plowman* B IX 105 'Wolde neuere þe feiþful fader his fiþele were vntempred', in addition to the alliteration on *f* the two words *feiþful* and *fiþele* share the consonant sequence *f–þ–l*. In cases like this it is not possible to tell whether the repetition of the other sounds was intended or not, for in an alliterative poem like *Piers Plowman* the law of probability suggests that there would be many occasions in which the alliterating words also shared other consonants. Rhyme or the echo of the final sounds of words appears almost as frequently as alliteration. We noted earlier the rhyme *hlynede ond dynede* in *Judith*. This type of sound effect was not confined to poetry, for prose writers like Richard Rolle who wanted to create a rich sound made use of it. Even in the more prosaic text, *John Gaytryge's Sermon* (1357), we find examples like the following:

> Ane es to consaile and wysse tham that are *wyll*. Another es to chasty tham that wyrkkys *ill*. The third es to solauce thaym that er sorowe*full* and comforthe thaym. The ferthe es to pray for thaym that ere syn*full*. The fyfte es to be tholemode when men mysdose *us*. The sexte es gladly to forgyffe when men haves grevede *us*: the sevend, when men askes us *for to here thaym*, if we cun mare than thay *for to lere thaym*.[15]

Other types of sound effect are found. The root of a word can be repeated with a different ending, which may be a different inflection or an ending of a different part of speech. In *Piers Plowman* B XVIII 2 'As a recchelees renk that recche þ of no wo,' the stem *recch(e)*- is found in both the adjective *recchelees* and the verb *recche þ*. Homophones were commonly used in rhyme as Chaucer did in the opening of *The General Prologue*:

> The hooly blisful martir for to seke,
> That hem hath holpen whan that they were seeke. (I. 17–18)

Sound effects may extend over a phrase or clause and do not have to be limited to single words. In such cases the pattern is based on similar stress pattern and syntax in which some words may be repeated. In 'Bute hwat tunghe mai hit telle, hwat heorte mai hit thenche . . .'[16] the syntactical framework is repeated, though the meaningful words are varied.

These examples in no way exhaust the many different kinds of jingle found in the literature of medieval England, though they give some idea of its attractiveness for medieval authors. Even these, however, raise a problem for the understanding of the texts, and that is how significant such effects were for the overall meaning of the text in which they occur. Opinion has varied from accepting that they were mechanical contrivances introduced because it was fashionable to do so to claiming that they were important to the author's meaning and were deliberately introduced to highlight significant words and to create different levels of meaning. It is not possible to give any general principle whereby all types of jingle may be understood within a medieval text, for it is far from certain that there was any uniformity in authorial practice at the time. There can be little doubt that even the best authors indulged in this type of word-play for sheer exuberance and for the pleasure of the resulting sounds. The echo of *seke:seeke* in *The General Prologue* was no doubt admired for its cleverness, though it is difficult to think that contemporary readers felt it added to the meaning of the passage. However, it is true that rhetorical tricks of this kind are often found in passages of greater emotional intensity, as is true of the final example quoted in the last paragraph, and were designed to heighten the emotion of those passages. Also at a time when punctuation was less grammatical than it is today, such effects could be used as aids to point passages and so they assisted the reader to understand the organization of the paragraph in which they occur, as seems to be true of the quotation from *John Gaytryge's Sermon*.

What is less certain is whether jingles by themselves were intended to provide ambiguity or different levels of meaning, though they could of course be used in conjunction with other rhetorical tricks to direct attention to certain words which might otherwise have further meaning. Medieval audiences took more pleasure in sound than we do, and it is probably wise to retain a degree of scepticism towards the claims that jingles are important for establishing the meaning and ambiguity of medieval texts. It is possible when Chaucer wrote in *Troilus and Criseyde* 'So whan this Calkas knew by calkulynge' (I. 71) that he meant the readers to assume that the name Calchas was linked in some way to astronomical calculation. But as that is not a feature of Calchas' nature which is stressed, it may be that Chaucer simply introduced the jingle here from pure love of word-play. To create hidden ambiguities and extension of meaning in jingles like this redounds in our opinion to a writer's credit, but it is unlikely that this view was common in the medieval period.

Repetition, a device recommended by the rhetoricians, is one of the foremost types of word-play used in the medieval period, though once again it is a form which we today take to less kindly. We have already seen some examples of this in the previous chapter. When the same word is repeated its meaning may change slightly in its several occurrences so that some degree of ambiguity may be present. In the following interchange between Reynard the fox and Bruin the bear in Caxton's *Reynard the Fox* the repetition of the word *mesure* occurs:

> And [Reynard] sayde to the bere all lawhyng 'See nou wel sharply to. In this tree is so moche hony that it is without mesure. Asaye yf ye can come therin; and ete but lytil for though the honycombes be swete and good, yet beware that ye

ete not to many. But take of them by mesure that ye cacche no
harme in your body, for, swete eme, I shold be blasmed yf they
dyde you ony harme.' 'What, Reynart cosyn, sorowe ye not for
me. Wene ye that I were a fole: mesure is good in alle mete?'[17]

The ambiguity in this passage arises more from the context than
from the meaning of the words, for Reynard has carefully brought
Bruin to this spot intending to deceive him. He knows the bear's
greed is such that it will become trapped in the tree-trunk. The use
of the word *mesure* helps to point to this underlying criticism of the
bear.

Extreme repetition is found in the thirteenth-century lyric *Erthe
upon Erthe*, a poem of considerable popularity if the extant manuscript versions are anything to go by. It may be that the lyric
started life as a short riddle poem which was gradually expanded by
later scribes, though the expanded versions are unable to maintain
the level of repetition found in the original stanza. The version of it
found in MS Harley 2253 is as follows:

> Erþe toc of erþe erþe wyþ woh,
> Erþe oþer erþe to þe erþe droh,
> Erþe leyde erþe in erþene þroh,
> þo heuede erþe of erþe erþe ynoh.[18]

The author's intention was clearly to introduce as many examples of
the word *erþe* as possible in this stanza and part of our pleasure
comes from recognizing his expertise in the handling of the language.
There is an element of wit here though it is relatively unsophisticated.

Perhaps more typical is the repetition of *colours* found in the
prologue to *The Franklin's Tale*:

> Colours ne knowe I none, withouten drede,
> But swiche colours as growen in the mede,
> Or elles swiche as men dye or peynte.
> Colours of rethoryk been to me queynte. (v. 723–6).

Unfortunately we today think of this type of linguistic juggling as
mere pedantry because little ambiguity and extension of meaning
are involved. Repetition over a much wider canvas, but basically of
the same type, is found in *Pearl* where the first and last lines of a
stanza are echoed in the subsequent stanzas within the same section
of the poem. The result can help to accentuate the meaning and
development of the poem, but the principal effect is of sheer verbal
artistry and dexterity. For this type of repetition is very artificial

and contrived; it is also quite apparent. There can be no question of our having to puzzle out the meaning of the words repeated, for the repetition per se does not add to the difficulty of understanding the poem.

Repetition of a different kind is found when a word is repeated in a slightly varied form. This kind, even more than the previous one, resembles the jingle, for the overall effect is one of an echoing of sound rather than a play on words. Typical is the repetition of *preamble* in various forms in the exchange between the Friar and the Summoner immediately before *The Wife of Bath's Tale*:

> "Now dame," quod he, "so have I joye or blis,
> This is a long preamble of a tale!"
> And whan the Somonour herde the Frere gale,
> "Lo," quod the Somonour, "Goddes armes two!
> A frere wol entremette hym everemo.
> Lo, goode men, a flye and eek a frere
> Wol falle in every dyssh and eek mateere.
> What spekestow of preambulacioun?
> What! amble, or trotte, or pees, or go sit doun!" (III. 830–8)

There is no extension of meaning involved here; the repetition is little more than exuberant play with words.

Repetition need not be quite so random as the previous examples may suggest, for it is frequently included within some rhetorical figure. The repetition of the same word at the beginning of succeeding lines of poetry or at identical places in prose clauses or sentences will normally imply that the author is following some rhetorical precept. This is true of the famous example in *Troilus and Criseyde* v 1828–32:

> Swich fyn hath, lo, this Troilus for love!
> Swich fyn hath al his grete worthynesse!
> Swich fyn hath his estat real above,
> Swich fyn his lust, swich fyn hath his noblesse!
> Swich fyn hath false worldes brotelnesse!

Passages like this are common in both Old and Middle English and it would be otiose to quote further examples. All we need to remark is how deliberate and open the word-play is – as is characteristic of most occurrences of word-play in medieval English.

Another type of word-play was that which approaches our own punning, in which two meanings of a word might be implied at the same time so that the concealed meaning might be used in a play on some other word or idea. A good example comes from the fourteenth-century drinking song *Fill Every Glass*:

> Iff þe butlers name be water,
> I wold he were a galow-claper,
> but if he bryng vs drynk þe raþer.[19]

Here there is a pun on *water* and *Walter*, for the drinkers want Walter to provide them with beer or wine rather than with water. A further example is provided by another fourteenth-century lyric, *Love in the Garden*, which needs to be quoted in full:

> I haue a new gardyn,
> & newe is be-gunne;
> swych an-oþer gardyn
> know I not vnder sunne.
>
> In þe myddis of my gardyn
> is a peryr set,
> & it wele non per bern
> but a per Ienet.
>
> þe fayrest mayde of þis toun
> preyid me,
> for to gryffyn her a gryf
> of myn pery tre.
>
> quan I hadde hem gryffid
> alle at her wille,
> þe wyn & þe ale
> che dede in fille.
>
> & I gryffid her
> ryȝt vp in her home;
> & be þat day xx wowkes
> it was qwyk in her womb.
>
> þat day twelfus month,
> þat mayde I mette:
> che seyd it was a per robert,
> but non per Ionet![20]

The lover has grafted his pear tree onto his beloved so that she produced no John fruit (the name of a pear), but Robert fruit (the name of the child that was born). We may note two things about these puns. The first is that they both occur in lyrics and the second that they both involve personal names which are themselves of foreign origin. Because lyrics are short and often lead to a verbal climax, it is easy enough to make a pun of this kind which could be preserved even under the conditions of medieval copying. No doubt scribes expected lyrics to contain some kind of linguistic wit. The relative scarcity of short poems and lyrics in medieval England, particularly those of a secular nature, may be one reason why puns are much less common in our medieval literature and why ambiguity is so rare. The use of personal names or foreign words would help the pun to stand out. Since medieval lyrics generally deal with nameless lovers or adventurers, the introduction of a name would draw the reader's attention and alert him to a possible word-play. When that name occurs at the end of the lyric, few could mistake the point of the poem. That words of foreign origin are involved may be a sign that some of these puns were taken over from French lyrics. It does not of course follow that all puns in Middle English are found under these conditions, though many of them are.

This brief chapter has not been able to do justice to the complexities of a fascinating topic, and I have not had time to consider the question of pronunciation which is so important in deciding which words may have sounded alike. I have been content to try and reach some general conclusions. As a rule in medieval literature we find jingles, repetition and other kinds of play on sounds more frequently than they occur today. Conversely modern types of ambiguity are rarely encountered. The two most important reasons for this state of affairs in the medieval period are that rhetorical figures involving sound effects were encouraged by the traditional handbooks on rhetoric and that the language was not standardized or stable. The most stable sounds in the language were the consonants, and they were the ones which participated most frequently in the sound effects. Alliteration was principally a consonantal metre, for all vowels and diphthongs were treated as the same sound. Since alliterating sounds occurred at the beginning of words they were preserved more readily across dialect boundaries and from one century to the next, because much greater variety existed in the final unstressed syllables. Rhyme which is based on the identity of vowel sounds is easily disturbed in English. If, for example, the words in the first lines of *Piers Plowman* are transliterated into modern English, they remain recognizably alliterative poetry. If the same thing is done to the opening of *The General Prologue* of *The*

Canterbury Tales, the result is disastrous. That medieval English poets should nevertheless have insisted on using rhyme, a form of metrical composition unsuited to the nature of the language, is an indication of the considerable prestige of Latin and French.

When sounds were repeated over several words, this could produce several results. It could make copying more accurate since the repetition of a sound was something which a scribe would readily notice and so seek to preserve. Similarly it would strike a reader and so lead him to pay closer attention to those passages in which the sound effects occurred. However, provided the repetition was on consonants and at the beginning of a word, modernization or even word-substitution could take place without disturbing the overall pattern. Thus either Old English *macode* or Modern English *made* participates freely in an alliteration on *m*. Similarly it would be possible to substitute *sleepy* for *slothful* and still preserve the *sl*-sound pattern without departing too far from the sense. This facility would be a great asset when poems were modernized or copied across dialect boundaries.

At the same time it must be accepted that concentration on sound effects in writing can, and usually does, lead to greater emphasis being placed on larger sense units than the word. Individual words in such sound schemes will not carry the same weight of meaning which we give them today. The occurrence of jingles and other sound plays reinforces the conclusion of the previous chapter that phrases and sentences were more meaningful and important in medieval English literature than words. These embellishments are also what one might expect from the nature of medieval punctuation which was referred to in the third chapter. Where punctuation is more rhetorical than grammatical, sound effects will often help to accentuate the rhetorical units. It is, therefore, sensible to be sceptical towards modern suggestions about puns in medieval literature, unless they are carefully prepared and pointed out by the author through one of the means available to him. Particularly in longer poems the concealed pun should be discounted unless the evidence for its existence is strong. That we today have a penchant for ambiguity does not in itself make the occurrence of puns in medieval literature more likely.

6

Parody

TYPES OF PARODY

Although it is frequently claimed that both parody and satire were extensively practised in the medieval period, I have decided in this chapter to limit my attention to the former, for the latter has already been dealt with by Professor Peter.[1] In his book he suggested that satire was an attack directed at named objects or people; it is personal and particular. Complaint, the true medieval genre, was concerned with general abuse rather than with personal idiosyncrasies. Its target was not so much individuals as society as a whole – and this is a feature which is reflected in the language used in such works. In this chapter I will suggest that a similar situation exists between parody and burlesque in medieval English literature.

Parody was rarely used in our period when burlesque was the characteristic form. It is essential to understand how the two types differ. Parody is the ridiculing of a particular turn of expression, work or genre by imitating its characteristic linguistic features and either modifying them slightly or applying them to ridiculous ends. Burlesque, on the other hand, makes use of current literary conventions and genres to poke fun at social aspirations and ideals without necessarily intending any mockery to fall on the literary forms so exploited. Burlesque looks beyond literature to society, whereas the goal of parody does not go beyond the belittling of a particular literary work or type. Burlesque is general and parody is particular. Finally, and most importantly for our purposes, burlesque is more concerned with attitudes than with language, whereas the very heart of parody is the exploitation and echoing of linguistic features.

It follows from this definition and from what was written in earlier chapters of this book that certain types of parody could not be practised in medieval English. As there was no such thing as a received text of any literary work, it was impossible to parody a particular work. As the words of texts changed through copying, it would not be possible for a parodist to evoke the words of a poem to

ridicule it. The constant modernization of language to which medieval texts were subject would preempt the need for parody, since all
literature available would be written in the current literary styles.
We saw in the first chapter how literary echoes were weak because it
was impossible to imitate the exact words of the model. Similarly
authors referred to the deeds of heroes in a general way rather than
to the particular expression of those exploits in a given work,
because there was insufficient stability in the individual works. The
same limitations apply to parody and made the belittling of individual works impossible. If, for example, Chaucer's *Sir Thopas* is a
parody, it is not one of a *particular* romance, only of a *type* of
romance. It should not be assumed from this that Englishmen were
ignorant of the possibilities of the effectiveness of literary echoes.
But in medieval England only Latin and French works acquired that
level of familiarity which made imitation possible; English ones
never did. Thus when in 1322 Edward II's favourite, Piers Gaveston,
was executed, the Latin poem exulting in his death which begins

> Pange, lingua, necem Petri
> qui turbavit Angliam

contains a clear echo of the famous hymn of Venantius Fortunatus
(*c.* 530–600) which opens *Pange, lingua, gloriosi*.[2] The fourteenth-
century poem is not by my definition a parody of the hymn, but its
imitation of the earlier hymn shows what possibilities were available
in Latin, which were closed to those who wrote in English. It is
hardly surprising that expressions of dissatisfaction with English
became common at the end of the medieval period.

It was not only the individual work which could not be parodied;
it was also individual turns of phrase, for there are in medieval
English few expressions which could be classified as individual. In
an age when writing was either formulaic or imitative, it is virtually
impossible to distinguish one writer's style from another's. Consequently it was not possible to parody an author; only general styles
could be ridiculed. Those who wished to indulge in parody faced the
perennial problem of degree. If one wants to expose the absurdities
of a particular style, one does so by exaggerating its characteristic
features so that the style appears ridiculous. But the readers of the
parody have to realize that the stylistic excesses represent ridicule
rather than a development of that particular style. For example,
formula and cliché are features of Old English poetic composition.
To parody this style the number of formulae and clichés can be
increased until the lines become so overloaded that the result is
absurd. The problem is, however, that it is a subjective assessment

deciding when that position is reached. As we today have a generally unfavourable attitude towards formulaic construction and 'poetic' language, we too readily assume that a few extra formulae are sufficient to transform certain works into parodies.

In periods when lexical extravagance met with widespread approval, it would be more difficult for a potential parodist to convince his contemporaries that he was composing a parody. Consider the opening lines of the prologue to the play *The Pride of Life*, probably written in the middle of the fourteenth century:

> Pees, and herkynt hal ifer,
> Ric and por, yong and hold,
> Men and wemen þat bet her,
> Bot lerit and leut, stout and bold.[3]

As far as I am aware it has never been suggested that these lines form a parody of the style they are written in – and it is not my intention to do so now. What I want to emphasize is that the last three lines of this stanza consist of various circumlocutions and clichés for the audience. To us the result is tedious, repetitive and bombastic; and we could be easily persuaded that this stanza was intended as a parody of that style which relied on uncritical use of such clichés. There is, I repeat, no evidence that this passage was intended or accepted as a parody. If, however, it was possible for an author to assemble three lines of repetitive clichés in an honest attempt at writing in the elevated style, how many lines were needed to make an audience aware that a parody of this kind of bombast was involved? Parodies might easily become but pale shadows of the original style. There is no easy answer to this question, though it is clear that exaggeration by itself is an insufficient guide to parody. This is a dictum that may apply in all ages; it is particularly true in medieval English literature. What is required is an indication from the author that parody is involved. Without that indication we should disregard modern identifications of possible parodies in Middle English. Although Chaucer refers in apparently uncomplimentary terms to the 'rum, ram, ruf' of the alliterative style, he uses alliteration in some battle scenes as, for example, in the tournament in *The Knight's Tale*. It would be quite possible for a modern critic to suggest that Chaucer was there parodying the alliterative style. As he gives no indication that he is indulging in parody, we have to reject any suggestion of this kind. Without the ability to pinpoint a particular work or author through language, much of the point of parody would be absent and so we may accept that it was a form without much appeal for writers in English in the Middle Ages.

The problem of degree in stylistic parody is not confined to the Middle Ages. The love of swelling bombast continued in the sixteenth and early seventeenth centuries. Thomas Wilson in his *Arte of Rhetorique* from 1553 printed a letter he had composed, which is so extravagant in its verbosity that it has become famous. Wilson wrote after this letter: 'Some will thinke and sweare it too, that there was neuer any such thing written . . . but I will say thus much, and abide by it too, the like haue been made heretofore, and praised aboue the Moon.'⁴ He was quite right, for many writers did use an exotic vocabulary and inflated syntax to make their English sound more elegant and weighty.⁵ Wilson failed to inform his readers how they could tell that his letter was a parody, for he claimed that it conformed to the stylistic norm of his time. In some respects parody was easier to detect in the Renaissance because people were more self-conscious about style, writers expatiated on their reasons for putting pen to paper, and there was far more of the kind of literary in-fighting which breeds parody. In the medieval period when authors revealed themselves and their intentions rarely, if at all, parody is more difficult to detect. More recently parody has been directed at individual books or authors in a quite specific way. When Max Beerbohm wrote a parody of Conrad's style, he based it directly on one of Conrad's works, *The Lagoon*.⁶ The reader who knows Conrad instantly recognizes the allusion and automatically adjusts his reactions to enjoy a parody. Our knowledge of the precise words used by an author and our feeling for tradition enable us to understand the parody without any deliberate introduction by the parodist to put his readers in the picture.

CHAUCER AND PARODY

Of all medieval English authors it is Chaucer upon whom modern critics have mainly fathered supposed parodies. Such a state of affairs is understandable since his literary output was considerable, his more objective attitude towards composition is well-known, and modern interest in the medieval period centres on him. Critical attention to parody in *The Canterbury Tales* has concentrated on *The Tale of Melibee* and *Sir Thopas*, both tales related by Chaucer the pilgrim. The former tale was his second attempt at a story after his tale about *Sir Thopas* had been interrupted because his audience could stand it no longer. *Melibee* is in prose and in this it resembles *The Parson's Tale*. It too has much of the sermon about it, since it is a didactic piece, and is a translation from French. Chaucer kept very close to his French source except that he tended to pad out his English by introducing doublets or parallel phrases and clauses not found there. The result is a much wordier piece, though the vocabulary

and syntax are not complicated by fourteenth-century standards; indeed they are simpler than those found in *The Parson's
Tale*. Many modern readers find *The Tale of Melibee* tiresome, partly
because of the subject matter with which we are no longer in tune,
partly because it is less amusing than most of the other tales, and
partly because we read so little Middle English prose. Recently
Professor Elliott has suggested that Chaucer was attempting to
parody the style of didactic prose without necessarily attacking the
moral message of the tale. He writes concerning its style and purpose
'There are three possibilities regarding this tale: first, that Chaucer
could not do any better; secondly, that he thought this mode of
writing it appropriate and effective, perhaps even beautiful; thirdly,
that he was being funny.'[7] No one regards the first possibility as at
all likely. Until recently most scholars assumed that the second was
the right one;[8] and now Professor Elliott suggests that the third
should be accepted. This attempt to understand *Melibee* as a parody,
and Professor Elliott is not alone in his view,[9] brings into focus the
point I have made in this chapter. If one critic can regard a medieval
work as a serious attempt at a particular style and another as a
parody of that style, then the boundary between a style and its
parody is very vague. It would have been as difficult for medieval
readers as it is for modern ones to decide whether they were reading
a straight piece of a parody. Without some clear indication by the
author, therefore, parody must be discounted.

As there is no such indication in *Melibee* I cannot accept Professor
Elliott's view. His claim is based on the fact that in comparison with
its French original Chaucer's *Melibee* is more wordy. We must remember that few, if any, of his audience were familiar with the French
original, and it is unlikely that any contemporary reader compared
the two versions. The audience would appreciate the style of the tale
by comparing it (perhaps subconsciously) with other prose pieces
known to them, including of course *The Parson's Tale*. If it is a
parody, it must be a parody of English didactic writing, for which
comparison with its French original is inappropriate. If it is a parody,
it has to be compared with other fourteenth-century didactic works.
As Elliott himself points out, the syntax in *Melibee* is less contrived
and the diction simpler than those found even in *The Parson's Tale*,
so that if the former was intended as a parody of the convoluted
didactic style it is difficult to know how a contemporary reader
realized this since *The Parson's Tale* was not. To accept Elliott's
view we have to assume not only that the style of English prose
didactic works was sufficiently homogeneous and distinctive that it
was recognized as such by contemporaries, but also that its characteristic features could readily be exaggerated to produce parody

Both are unlikely. The style of a work like Chaucer's *Melibee* was greatly influenced by its French original, as were many of the poetic tales in *The Canterbury Tales*. The use of heavy foreign words, of complicated syntax, and of rhetorical features like balance and parallelism was as commonly found in Chaucer's poetry as in his prose. In this *Melibee* differs little from non-Chaucerian prose as well, for that too was frequently adapted from foreign sources. There may have been different levels of style, as we shall see in a later chapter, but it seems improbable that medieval readers distinguished between the styles of different genres. It is difficult to claim that there was a courtly prose style as distinct from a religious prose style. *Melibee* is written in the high style, which is French-inspired, and that style was the fashionable one of the period. As a style it tends towards extravagance, and many examples of it in both Chaucer and other writers are far more elaborate than *Melibee*. To contemporaries the tale and its style can have seemed in no way exceptional. Finally, it should be noted that *Melibee* appears as a complete work divorced from the rest of *The Canterbury Tales* in at least five manuscript anthologies. From the other pieces in those anthologies one can deduce that their compilers thought *Melibee* was a serious piece seriously written. We would be mistaken to understand it in any other way.

The question of parody in *Melibee* is illuminated by *Sir Thopas*, but before turning to that tale I would like to consider another Chaucerian poem which has recently been categorized as parody. The *balade* usually known as *To Rosemounde* was until recently regarded as 'a typical complimentary poem in the spirit of courtly love',[10] but in their book the Spearings have taken it to be a parody.[11] As the poem is brief, it may be helpful to quote it in full.

> Madame, ye ben of al beaute shryne
> As fer as cercled is the mapemounde,
> For as the cristal glorious ye shyne,
> And lyke ruby ben your chekes rounde.
> Therwith ye ben so mery and so jocounde
> That at a revel whan that I see you daunce,
> It is an oynement unto my wounde,
> Thogh ye to me ne do no daliaunce.
>
> For thogh I wepe of teres ful a tyne,
> Yet may that wo myn herte nat confounde;
> Your seemly voys, that ye so smal outtwyne,
> Maketh my thoght in joye and blis habounde.
> So curtaysly I go, with love bounde,

> That to myself I sey, in my penaunce,
> "Suffyseth me to love you, Rosemounde,
> Thogh ye to me ne do no daliaunce."
>
> Nas never pyk walwed in galauntyne
> As I in love am walwed and ywounde,
> For which ful ofte I of myself devyne
> That I am trewe Tristam the secounde.
> My love may not refreyd be nor affounde;
> I brenne ay in an amorous plesaunce.
> Do what you lyst, I wyl your thral be founde,
> Thogh ye to me ne do no daliaunce.

The Spearings argue there are certain stylistic incongruities which indicate that this poem is a parody. In the first stanza the cheeks, rather than as usually in Middle English literature the lips, are described as ruby. In the second the poet sheds a tubful of tears and the lady has a rather thin voice, images which are out of keeping with the courtly tone. In the third the image of the pike is ludicrous, the comparison of the lover with Tristram exaggerated, and his insistence on being her thrall petulant.

The arguments here are of a more detailed linguistic nature than those advanced in the case of *Melibee*. Nevertheless, they can be reduced to two general principles. The first is that certain expressions were so well known that any deviation from them implies parody. The second is that in a literature full of stock images, any image which goes beyond the normal range is exaggerated and therefore parodistic. I find it difficult to accept either idea in those poems where the author fails to include some indication of his intentions, as is true of *To Rosemounde*. Whether 'ruby cheeks' were so unusual in late Middle English that the phrase could be considered a perversion of 'ruby lips' is itself debatable. Quite apart from this specific point, the general principle is unlikely in view of the situation then prevailing as to the scribal copying of manuscripts. In an age when literature was formulaic, there was a natural tendency for scribes to emend the language of the texts they were copying to the formulae known to them. If 'ruby lips' was so customary, one would imagine that Adam or one of his fellows would have replaced 'ruby cheeks' with 'ruby lips'. For unless the scribe was aware that a parody was in question (and he might find it difficult to appreciate this when the author failed to inform him of it), he would be offended by the formulaic lapse and he would correct his copy. Authors would be aware of this state of affairs which would act as a constraint upon their linguistic freedom.

The same applies to the exaggerated images. The courtly love environment was one that encouraged exaggeration, for each new hero has to be presented as more in love than the previous one. There was a natural inflation in both language and imagery, for how else is the poet to persuade us of the great love he or his fictional lover feels. It is unlikely, therefore, that the images appeared as incongruous then as they do now. Chaucer may have exercised his ingenuity in his choice of images, but that does not mean he was writing a parody. The language of the time was not sufficiently subtle to enable poets to create such ingenious contrasts and incongruities. When an author wanted to pervert current conventions, he was forced to do so blatantly. The following fifteenth-century attack on women, for example, really does stand accepted attitudes upside down:

> Youre Camusyd nose, with nose-thryllys brode,
> Vnto the chyrch a noble Instrument
> To quenche tapers brennyng afore the roode,
> ys best apropyed at myne avysament;
> your leud lokyng, doble of entent,
> wyth courtly loke al of saferon hew,
> That neuer wol fayle – þe colour is so trew![12]

Chaucer's *balade*, however, exhibits the exaggeration typical of its genre, though that exaggeration is expressed in somewhat unusual images. But the unusual images are themselves typical of the infla-tion of imagery. Consequently the language of this poem does not justify us in taking it as a parody. It is difficult to see how an audience accustomed to the blatant distortions of *The Lover's Mock-ing Reply*, a stanza from which I have just quoted, could adjust themselves to take *To Rosemounde* as parody.

Sir Thopas, however, is the one tale by Chaucer universally accepted as a parody. It is important to realize that there are certain features of this tale which make it quite different from others in *The Canterbury Tales*. The first of these is that the tale was interrupted by the Host so it remained unfinished. This incompleteness was essential if the tale was to be taken as a parody, for if it had been completed it could easily have been abstracted from its context and passed off as a straight tale. As it stands, *Sir Thopas* can be apprecia-ted only in the light of its context, particularly the words of the Host. I therefore find it difficult to accept, as is often suggested, that Chaucer got tired of his parody and so failed to complete it. Never-theless, the tale's incompleteness has to be taken in conjunction with the second feature, the comments by Harry Bailey. It is not unusual for him to comment on a tale; but this is the only occasion where his comments are so unfavourable and he brings a tale to a premature conclusion. He refers to the teller's *lewednesse*, *drasty speche* and *rym dogerel*, though he does not explain what he means by those terms. It would, however, be clear to the reader from the Host's comments that there was something wrong with the tale, though it would be interesting to know how many of them were surprised by the Host's reaction for they had been led by him to expect *som deyntee thyng* (VII. 711). Chaucer's contemporaries were used to reading or hearing exotic and exaggerated stories translated from French, and many may have taken *Sir Thopas* in this spirit before being informed otherwise by the Host. It is by setting the story within the context of the comments of the Host that Chaucer is able to underline its character. The third feature is the choice of metre, for *Sir Thopas* is written in a metre which imitates that found in the tail-rhyme romances and it is the only tale in *The Canterbury Tales* in this metre. Although there is no uniformity of metre in *The Canterbury Tales* and some tales are in prose, we may have here an attempt to suggest the nature of the tale by its metre. We need not think that Chaucer necessarily felt tail-rhyme metre to be absurd; it is simply that it is different from the other metres in the poem and so attracts attention.

As is typical of other Middle English parodies there is no echo or ridiculing of other individual Middle English works. It has, however, been suggested that Chaucer was familiar with the Auchinleck manuscript which contained a whole range of romances, most of which were translated from French sources.[13] The lines in *Sir Thopas*:

> Yet listeth, lordes, to my tale
> Murier than the nightyngale (VII. 833–4)

may be an echo of the lines in the Auchinleck version of *Beves of Hamtoun*:

> Lordinges, herkneþ to my tale
> Is merier þan þe niȝtingale.

While this supposition appears reasonable, Chaucer did not intend his audience to understand that particular echo in such a limited way. The number of people who knew the Auchinleck version was small, and Chaucer himself makes the echo less significant by including a similar request for hearing at the beginning of the poem, which uses different words:

> Listeth, lordes, in good entent,
> And I wol telle verrayment (VII. 712–13).

Most readers would have understood both these examples to be a parody of that kind of romance opening; they were hardly likely to have associated one of them with an opening in a particular romance. With reference to these two passages from *Sir Thopas* Professor Burrow has noted that Chaucer's usage is 'hearken' rather than 'listen', so that he deliberately suppressed his own usage in order to bring out the parody.[14] While this may be so, the change makes the suggested echo from the Auchinleck manuscript less obvious and, furthermore, a contemporary audience would not realize how Chaucer had modified his usage for they did not have the benefit of modern concordances. We cannot assume that a reader then would notice any change in Chaucer's normal usage and so understand that a parody was involved.

The crucial question remains what features of the language are there in *Sir Thopas* which indicate that a parody is present? The answer would seem to be that the words and constructions used are in themselves unexceptional and would not cause any comment in a straight romance. It is possible, as was suggested in the case of *To Rosemounde*, that certain words and expressions are used in an inappropriate context in *Sir Thopas* and thus indicate a humorous parody. When *Sir Thopas* is described as:

> Sire Thopas wax a doghty swayn;
> Whit was his face as payndemayn,
> His lippes rede as rose (VII. 724–6)

it has been claimed that a white face and red lips are more characteristic of a woman than of a knight who is described as a 'doghty swayn'. This is dubious, for in *The Romaunt of the Rose*, part of which is attributed to Chaucer, the lover is described as follows:

> His breth is also good and swete,
> And eke his lippis rody, and mete
> Oonly to pleyen and to kesse. (3743–5)

Indeed in an age of greater extravagance in personal adornment among both males and females, it may be doubted whether these lines would cause comment. Other possible absurdities and incongruities have been put forward. Thopas climbs into his saddle (797), whereas some commentators think he should have leapt or vaulted into it. He has *sydes smale* which suggests an effeminacy inappropriate in a knight. And so on. Most of these attempts to find incongruity are desperate, and few are convincing. It is difficult to escape the conclusion that there is nothing in the language of *Sir Thopas* to indicate that it is unusual as a tail-rhyme romance – and this may well have been Chaucer's message. The literary language of the period was not so well developed that a reader could regard 'climb' as significantly different in connotation from 'leap' or 'vault'. The parody is indicated from the outside by the words of the Host as he breaks off the tale, not from the inside by the language.

The nature of what can be regarded as normal Middle English parody is illustrated in the stanza already quoted from *The Lover's Mocking Reply*. In that poem there is an element of the grotesque achieved by perverting what would normally be expected in the circumstances. The lady does not have a dainty nose; on the contrary she sports a snub-nose with two large nostrils which could easily serve to blow out the candles in the church. There is no attempt to create a gentle exaggeration in the language and there can be no doubt about the author's humorous intention. This type of distortion is common. *The Tournament of Tottenham* from the early fifteenth century contains the same kind of perversion, for instead of a chivalrous tournament fought by knights, we have a brawl fought by the locals. This is how they prepare themselves:

> þay armed ham in mattis:
> þay set on þer nollys,
> For to kepe þer pollys,
> Gode blake bollys,
> For batryng of battis.

> þay sowed þam in schepe-skynnes for þay suld not brest;
> Ilkon toke a blak hat insted of a crest,
> A harow brod as a fanne aboune on þer brest,
> And a flayle in þer hande, for to fyght prest.
>   Furth gon þay fare.[15]

The weapons and armour are those suited to the lower classes; they are not the accoutrement of knights. The author's *insted of a crest* illustrates this difference. A similar delight in the grotesque is exhibited in *The Land of Cokaygne* (c. 1275), in which there is an abbey whose walls are made of food, not stone:

> þer is a wel fair abbei
> Of white monkes and of grei.
> þer beþ bowris and halles,
> Alle of pasteiis beþ þe walles,
> Of fleis, of fisse and rich met,
> þe likfullist þat man mai et.

Fluren cakes beþ þe schingles alle
Of cherche, cloister, boure and halle,
þe pinnes beþ fat podinges,
Rich met to princeȝ and kinges.[16]

The poem contains many other delightful absurdities like this.

It is evident from these examples that no one could mistake the nature of these poems which were humorous corruptions and perversions of some of the popular ideas and conventions of the time. They gain their power by putting forward bizarre images which run counter to, and hence question, the accepted modes of thought and behaviour. Consequently these poems were more in the nature of burlesque than of parody, for they did not poke fun at a particular poem or even type of poem; they were aimed at social conventions and general literary expectations. The language in the poems is distorted only in the sense that they use low style to handle subjects which would normally be treated in the high style. The humour springs from the incongruity of the subject matter and the style; it is a very blatant and crude incongruity. The inherent tendency towards inflation in the high style meant that humour could come only from the use of low style, in unexpected situations, and not from exaggeration of the high style. The result is that ideas and general literary ideals are criticized rather than individual poems and forms of expression. It was difficult, if not impossible, to write parody in the way we know it today. Subtle exaggeration or direct echoes were out of the reach of parodists. They had to indicate their intentions externally as Chaucer did in *Sir Thopas* or blatantly by using another style. Consequently to avoid confusion it is simpler to think of burlesque, not parody, as the medieval genre.

7

Themes

In medieval English literature the individual word was less important than either phrase or theme; it is for this reason that a chapter on themes finds a place here. Some scholars understand 'theme' in the relatively restricted sense of an established *topos*, like that of the Old English beasts of battle, in which the same phrases and concepts will recur to express a common idea. In this chapter I use it in the other, wider sense, to which the paragraph is a modern equivalent except that medieval themes are limited to a more clearly defined set of subjects. The description of a castle is a theme, but each description will vary depending on the dialect and date of the work of literature, to say nothing of the purpose for which it is used. It is in this variety that theme differs from *topos*; examples are found later in the chapter. Themes then are like paragraphs in that they are the small structural units of composition, but they differ from them in being limited to a traditional range of subjects. Medieval authors created their stories by linking traditional themes in new patterns. The bricks used in construction were uniform, but the resulting houses varied widely in their overall design. This is how 'theme' is generally used by proponents of the oral-formulaic theory, though composition by theme need not prove oral composition since many themes in medieval English were borrowed from Latin or French and were thus literary rather than oral in character. It is my view that much of our medieval literature was composed by theme (though naturally varying in length, intention and conventionality) and that this method of composition was encouraged by the state of the language then.

Themes are neutral till given significance by an author either by explicit comment or by juxtaposition with other themes. A good example is the theme of feasting which can be made either noble and courtly or disgusting and debauched. In *Sir Gawain and the Green Knight* the feasting at Arthur's court exemplifies the civilized and excellent character of the knights of the Round Table. The picture of fashionable behaviour representing an ideal is accentuated by the noble games and courtly entertainments which precede the feasting. Quite the opposite picture is presented in the Old English *Judith* where the Assyrians are portrayed as wicked and loathsome. Holofernes and his men indulge themselves in too much food and drink so that the feast becomes an example of excess and sinfulness. It forms a fitting prelude to the attempted rape of Judith by Holofernes. There is nothing in feasting by itself which makes it either good or bad; the author provides it with the meaning appropriate for his own particular purpose. This point is worth remembering because in our enthusiasm for comparing one poem with another we are sometimes in danger of thinking that themes were so stereotyped that they were used uniformly by different authors. It is true that some historical and legendary figures such as Sigurd, Heremod and Theodoric were introduced into Old English poetry only in a good or a bad sense, but this state merely reflects the paucity of examples based on the exploits of these heroes in the extant literature. A poet could readily have used Heremod as an example of a good king by concentrating on his early life, just as Sigurd could have been made into an example of various kinds of sinfulness such as incest, pride or disloyalty.

We are wrong to think that stories of heroes and other legendary characters were so well known that writers and readers could react to them in only one set way. The example of Troy shows that this is not so. Accounts written from the Greek and Trojan point of view were well known in the Middle Ages which necessarily meant that the participants in the siege could be viewed in almost totally opposed ways. The point is made by Caxton in the epilogue of his *History of Troy* (1473–4):

> For dyverce men have made dyverce bookes whiche in all poyntes acorde not, as Dictes, Dares and Homerus. For Dictes and Homerus, as Grekes, sayn and wryten favorably for the Grekes and gyve to them more worship than to the Trojans. And Dares wryteth otherwyse than they doo.[1]

He was not the only one aware of this discrepancy. Nevertheless, certain themes, such as the *Ubi sunt* theme which laments the passing of people and things from this world, were used only in a limited number of ways, though even this theme was invested with quite divergent tones varying from the elegiac to the exultant. Naturally some themes such as that of the tyrannical king appeared only in those places where an author wanted to present a character of that type; such themes are necessarily restricted in application.

One of the effects of composition by theme was that characters are used as supports for the story rather than as models of psychological consistency. This is one reason for the startling examples of *volte face* in medieval literature. In the late fourteenth-century romance *Athelston* the king is portrayed at first as a noble ruler. When he learns of Egeland's supposed treachery, he is metamorphized into the familiar inhuman tyrant who in this case acts like a madman and kicks his pregnant wife in the stomach so that their child is stillborn. Convinced of Egeland's innocence he turns once again into a noble king who is unwilling to break his oath or act unjustly. The portrayal of the king in one theme is quite contrary to his representation in another, for such themes were designed to promote the narrative and not for the internal cohesion of the characters. The example is clear enough in a poem of lesser critical stature, but this use of theme is just the same in the better poems, where we are in danger of overlooking it.

A good example is provided by Gawain's preparation for departure from Bercilak's castle in *Sir Gawain and the Green Knight*. During the lady's third visit to his bedroom Gawain accepts her green girdle to protect his life at the Green Chapel and agrees not to surrender it to her husband, thus breaking his obligation under the rules of the exchange of winnings. As soon as the lady leaves he gets up, dresses, and goes to the chapel where he hears mass, confesses and is given absolution of all his sins. It was a conventional theme that a man about to embark on a journey involving his probable death heard mass and was confessed. There are, however, two ways of looking at this episode. The first is that the poet introduced these details as part of his theme of the preparation for departure to build up suspense because the theme implies the hero's probable death. As a result he was unconcerned, or even unaware, of the incongruity and impropriety of Gawain's behaviour at this stage. The handling of this theme recalls the way Bercilak himself attends mass before going hunting as part of the theme of early morning departure, for it might be considered just as incongruous that Bercilak should attend mass in view of the fact that he is a shape-changer whom some scholars associate with the devil. The second is that the poet introduced the details of Gawain's mass and confession deliberately as a comment on his behaviour. As Professor Burrow remarks: 'There is – there must be! – irony in the application of eulogistic epithets to Gawain during this discreditable period (unless ironies are to be sought with still greater difficulty in the later descriptions of his remorse).'[2] It is claimed that the poet developed Gawain in a psychologically consistent manner and that both to refer to him by eulogistic epithets and to let him be absolved when he is in a state of sin can be understood only as an exercise in irony. The best authors, so this view implies, are so concerned with consistency in plot and character that themes which seem inappropriate are introduced to strike a discordant note. This view raises the question whether medieval writers and readers understood that themes could be ironic by containing elements which ran counter to their normal expectations – a question to which I shall turn in a moment.

The ease with which we misunderstand how themes were used by medieval authors can be illustrated by another example from *Sir Gawain and the Green Knight*. At the beginning of the poem the courtiers at Arthur's court are feasting after the festivities of the day. Suddenly the Green Knight enters and everyone falls silent. The Arthurian knights gaze at him in amazement and some creep nearer to see what he is going to do. Although the court had witnessed many marvels, this man was the most unusual ever seen there. Some modern critics see in this silence of the knights an ironic comment on the courtly ethos as exemplified by Arthur and his men, and they suggest that the poet is here laughing at their chivalric pretensions because as soon as any real danger appears they behave like frightened children. When presented in this way, this view seems plausible, although it is little short of absurd. It presupposes that the knights at court should have turned round to see what the noise was, said to one another 'Oh, it's only a green knight', and then carried on eating their dinner. On the contrary, the poet is here employing the theme of amazement in order to create dramatic suspense with the Green Knight's entrance. It is used for narrative purposes which have nothing to do with ironic comments on Arthur's court, for as already stated themes were used to develop the story, not to create internal consistency in the presentation of character. This theme is not unlike that of the beasts of battle which figures so frequently in Old English poetry. Both are used to create the emotional atmosphere associated with some impending event: the one a battle in which many men will die, the other some marvellous combat or duel as yet unexplained. For although there is a strong narrative in most Old and Middle English poems, many of their themes not only assist the progress of the story, but also create the atmosphere associated with that story.

Two interrelated problems which arise from the discussion so far are: how did a writer inject significance into his themes and to what extent were small differences in the handling of a theme, as for example the replacement of usual words or rhetorical embellishments by less usual ones, of importance in getting across the significance the author intended? In general, themes gained their significance by being contrasted or associated with other themes and from their place in the story in which they occur. The use of some traditional themes in Chaucer's *Troilus and Criseyde* was examined by R. O. Payne in his *The Key of Remembrance*.³ Payne notes how the first three books make frequent use of the spring and spring-flowers theme so that there is a cumulative effect in them of lightness, gaiety and love. The later books are contrasted with the first three by their use of the winter theme which gives them a more sombre and chilling atmosphere. In each case the theme and the way it is handled are highly conventional: the vocabulary and the rhetoric are traditional; but taken together the themes provide an atmosphere for the working out of the plot. The implication is that neither author nor audience paid close attention to the individual words or phrases forming the theme, but absorbed its general effect which was then contrasted or associated with other themes of a similar kind. The theme acquires its force from this link with other themes rather than from the way in which it is put together itself. The theme of the seasons is handled in much the same way by the author of *Sir Gawain and the Green Knight*, and a similar effect is achieved by the digressions in *Beowulf* which provide a heroic backcloth to the action. The heroes mentioned in them are either compared or contrasted with Beowulf himself so that he is measured against them. In these digressions it is not of importance which particular hero is chosen for illustrative purposes or even how the hero is presented in detail, just as in *Troilus and Criseyde* Chaucer could have chosen a different series of themes to provide the atmospheric background for his story. Each hero becomes part of a larger thematic pattern. The important point is that although themes were handled in conventional ways they could nevertheless be grouped in significant patterns, and it was this grouping rather than the choice of words or phrases within a theme which provided the atmosphere and tone of a work of art.

In order to discuss the content of a theme and its purpose I would like to quote two examples from the so-called *Ubi sunt* theme, the theme which contrasts the vanished glories of the past with the poverty of the present. The first is the well-known example from the Old English *The Wanderer*:

> Hwær cwom mearg? Hwær cwom mago? Hwær cwom maþþumgyfa?
> Hwær cwom symbla gesetu? Hwær sindon seledreamas?
> Eala beorht bune! Eala byrnwiga!
> Eala þeodnes þrym! Hu seo þrag gewat,
> genap under nihthelm, swa heo no wære. (92–6)

(What has become of the horse? What has become of the kinsman? What has become of the glorious lord? What has become of the banqueting halls? What has become of the feasting in the hall? Alas the gleaming goblet! Alas the armed warrior! Alas the prince's glory! How that time has disappeared, grown dark under cover of night as though it never was.)

The second is from the less familiar Middle English translation, *The Book of Vices and Virtues* (*c.* 1375), of the French text *Somme le Roi*:

And that witnesseth wel the kynges, the erles, the prynces and the emperoures, that hadde sum tyme the joye of the world, and now thei lyen in helle and crien and wailen and waryen [curse] and seyn: 'Alas, what helpeth now us oure londes, oure grete power in erthe, honoures, nobeleye, joye and bost? Al is passed – ye, sonner than a schadewe or foul fleynge or a quarel of an arblawst [bolt from a cross-bow]; and thus passeth oure lif: now be we bore and thus sone dede.[4]

Both these passages lack specific reference. It would be difficult to tell where they came from if that information was not already available, for themes are universal. There is no attempt to localize them in time or place, and in this they resemble complaint as against satire and burlesque as against parody. The two passages are coloured only by the social conditions operating at the time they were written, since what is most admired at any one time is that which will figure in a list of what has passed. To the Anglo-Saxon the passing of kinsmen and the lord who gives treasure were worth comment since these were the features of life which were highly valued. To the Middle English author lands, power and titles seemed more important and so were the more missed. This is, however, a very general framework of social desiderata on which to hang the *Ubi sunt* theme. One does not feel that the poet of *The Wanderer* necessarily had lost these things or that he considered the things he lists as inherently more important than the things which other Old English poets listed in comparable themes. In *The Wanderer*, for example, there is no reference to friends, though we know that friends were highly valued in that society. Similarly the poet does not include kings or emperors in his list, unless one interprets *mappumgyfa* to mean one or the other, but both figure specifically in a similar passage in *The Seafarer*. It must, I think, be accepted that writers included in their examples within the *Ubi sunt* theme items which appealed to the society in which they lived, but that the choice among the many items which could appear was random, dictated possibly by metrical considerations.

Not all themes allowed such a wide range of choice as the *Ubi sunt* theme. The beasts of battle theme in Old English poetry normally contains only three animals: the eagle, the wolf and the raven. It was not obligatory to introduce all three or even to refer specifically to the type of bird or animal present. The example in *The Battle of Maldon* includes only the raven and the eagle:

> þær wearð hream ahafen, hremmas wundon,
> earn æses georn. (106–7)
> (There a clamour was raised; the ravens circled around, the eagle eager for food.)

In *The Wanderer* there is reference to a bird and the wolf, though the bird is not specified:

>   sumne fugel oþbær
> ofer heanne holm, sumne se hara wulf
> deaðe gedælde. (81–3)
> (The bird carried one off across the deep sea; the grey wolf hands one over to death.)

It cannot have been regarded as significant by author or audience that examples of the theme were not identical. Similarly in *Sir Gawain and the Green Knight*, after Gawain is told by Sir Bercilak that he has been deceived by his wife, Gawain introduces the theme of men deceived by women. The examples he cites are those of Adam, Solomon, Samson and David. All are good biblical examples; there are none from fiction or from more recent history. It is improbable that the choice of these particular four men was regarded as important. If one had been left out or if a different name had been included, it would not have made any difference to the way the audience understood the theme and to its significance in the passage as a whole.

I have approached the question of themes in this way in the hope that what I have written about the examples might appear uncontroversial. If I had begun by commenting on the choice of individual words within a theme, it would have been more difficult to choose examples to meet with general acceptance, because we are accustomed to attaching significance to individual words. Nevertheless, I hope that what has been written so far validates the statement made at the beginning of the chapter. For example, it is unlikely that either poet or audience regarded the word *maþþumgyfa* in the *Ubi sunt* passage in *The Wanderer* as being of any significance in itself. Provided it fitted the exigencies of the metre, any other word or phrase for 'giver of treasure' would be accepted as conveying the same meaning and emphasis. Themes are general and lack particularity. The words chosen formed part of this generalizing tendency; they blended unobtrusively with their surroundings. The themes were varied partly by the other themes with which they were linked and partly by the tone which the writer was able to create for them. This tone was achieved by the way in which the conventional ideas and vocabulary were arranged in rhetorical patterns, for it was such patterns which made a theme more or less distinctive in the work as a whole. Thus in the *Ubi sunt* passage in *The Wanderer* what a reader or listener would notice was how it is introduced with three phrasal units instead of the two normally found in a line of Old English poetry:

> Hwær cwom mearg? Hwær cwom mago? Hwær cwom
>   maþþumgyfa?[5]

This sense of 'threeness' is accentuated by the syntactic parallelism of the three units which creates a sense of expectation in that this threeness deviates from the normal pattern of an Old English alliterative line. This heightens the tone of the passage. The effect is achieved partly by the rhetorical arrangement of the 'line' and partly by the contrast of this line with other Old English lines; the individual words though not entirely without significance are of much less importance. It is the pattern rather than the individual word which counts.

The poet uses conventional words, phrases and ideas in his theme, but the way he elaborates them and makes them part of a wider pattern are important in a critical evaluation of a medieval work. Where traditional themes are employed there is the danger that authors will use the same words and expressions constantly, and the resulting uniformity prevents that subtle interplay of theme which is the hallmark of the conscious medieval artist. Laȝamon comes very close to this in his *Brut*. A translation of the Anglo-Norman *Roman de Brut* by Wace, his poem was written in the traditional English alliterative style. When a theme occurred in Wace which struck a responsive chord with Laȝamon, and it happened particularly with those concerning warfare and feasting, he elaborated his original by introducing the words which were frequently used to express that theme in English.[6] While the total effect is very English (unlike many translations made in Middle English), it is doubtful whether Laȝamon or his audience felt that these additions added any significance to the poem. One such theme expanded from Wace's Anglo-Norman, that of storms, is of some interest for it has recently been shown that storms formed a theme in Middle English alliterative poetry.[7] The theme was modelled for the most part on a similar theme found in Latin works, of which the most influential were probably the *Historia destructionis Troiae* of Guido de Columnis and Vergil's *Aeneid*. It might be argued in a case like this that the English poet deliberately chose traditional words and phrases to provide an echo of their Latin equivalents. The heightening of the theme would then be achieved by the framework of literary reference and lexical echoes, as is true for example in certain eighteenth-century phrases and themes. However, although we today can trace the classical origins of the theme, the storm scene had an independent history and development in English which made most examples of it very different in vocabulary and tone from its Latin origins. There are, furthermore, so many possible classical sources and the potential echoes from various sources are so jumbled together that it is unlikely an English audience associated any particular word or phrase with a classical one. At best the echo was a generalized one; it is improbable that English authors like Laʒamon chose their vocabulary in order to create echoes of Latin texts.

A theme was built up by the use of conventional vocabulary. Some themes, such as the storm theme just mentioned, may be associated only with certain kinds of poetry. Themes found normally in alliterative poetry will naturally use conventional language associated with the alliterative style. When Chaucer used the battle theme in *The Knight's Tale* and elsewhere he was forced to use more alliterative vocabulary than was otherwise common with him. Where the new style gave no help (for Chaucer's French models dealt with love rather than with war), the old style had to be annexed for a scene to have its full impact. Examples like this reveal how important the method of thematic composition was. Chaucer knew the sort of words that went with a battle scene and he used them; but there is nothing to show that individual words within the theme were of any significance.

In this chapter the examples I have used have been drawn from the better themes which were more frequently repeated and often elaborately decorated. Themes of this kind were naturally most conventional in vocabulary and treatment precisely because they were most familiar. While it might seem that there was greater lexical freedom in the handling of the lesser themes, the whole concept of thematic composition in medieval literature would itself mean that author and audience paid less attention to the linguistic details of a theme than to its rhetorical embellishment and tone, its place in the story and its overall effect. We today should do the same.

8

Syntax

GENERAL CONSIDERATIONS

Modern accounts of medieval English syntax necessarily arrange the available material into general rules and trends, and so unwittingly create the impression that the language at the time was more regulated and systematic than it was. While all languages exhibit patterns to assist communication, it is often easier to detect those patterns in speech rather than in writing, which is subject to so many pressures pushing it in different directions. It is difficult to frame syntactic rules for Old and Middle English which cover all the extant examples, for all our evidence of the medieval language comes from written sources and the texts generally used for syntactic investigation are literary ones which are particularly subject to diverse influences. Modern investigations have the inherent danger that they create norms of linguistic use for medieval language which are then used by editors to emend their texts to make them conform to those norms. The result can be that the norms become self-perpetuating and self-justifying.

Within the framework of the written language two important influences in the medieval period are usually given insufficient weight in modern investigations; they are translation and copying. Both distort what might be called the 'natural' syntax of the language, particularly at a time when foreign works were considered normative and when there were no taught norms of syntax within the vernacular which could act as a restraint upon foreign influence. Even today when we read a modern translation it is often possible to tell that the work is translated because it contains certain un-English constructions. In the medieval period the borrowing of foreign constructions was a daily occurrence, for the majority of Old and Middle English authors took their subject matter and style from foreign works. The influence of translation can be felt either through the introduction of constructions which otherwise do not exist in English, such as the Latin ablative absolute, or by the imitation of foreign syntactic patterns in a rather less blatant way. In the ninth century Alfred in his translation of the *De consolatione philosophiae* by Boethius wanted to imitate the complex Latin verb forms and to do so relied on *sceolde* as a kind of auxiliary:

> þa he ða ðider com, ða sceolde cuman ðære helle hund ongean hine, þæs nama wæs Ceruerus, se sceolde habban þrio heafdu, ond onfægnian mid his steorte ond plegian wið hine for his hearpunga. Ða wæs ðær eac swiðe egeslic geatweard, ðæs nama sceolde bion Caron . . .[1]
>
> (When he came there, the hound of hell whose name was Cerberus and who had three heads came to meet him. Cerberus welcomed him by wagging his tail and fawned on him on account of his harping. There was a terrible porter called Charon.)

The result seems to us today atypical of Old English, although we cannot readily assess how far what we consider to be typical Old English constructions were themselves influenced by Latin constructions. Certainly when Alfred was writing his preface to the *Cura pastoralis*, which was a free composition, there can be little doubt that some of his involved sentences were the result of a desire to imitate the style of Latin:

> For ðon ic ðe bebiode ðæt ðu do swæ ic geliefe ðæt ðu wille ðæt ðu ðe ðissa woruldðinga to ðæm geæmetige, swæ ðu oftost mæge, ðæt ðu ðone wisdom ðe ðe God sealde ðær ðær ðu hiene befæstan mæge, befæste.[2]
>
> (And so I command you to behave as I believe you will by freeing yourself from the things of this world as often as you can so that you employ that wisdom which God bestowed upon you wherever you may put it to best use.)

The question that arises from an example like this is how far the constructions involved are Old English ones. How many other examples of such a concentration of verbs at the end of a sentence are required to indicate that the construction was 'natural' in Old English? Questions of this sort may not be appropriate, for authors who could write like this perhaps had no sense of what was English syntax and what was not. To some extent it could be said that any syntactic construction in written English was acceptable provided it had a model in some other language. Yet a modern syntax of Old English will naturally suggest that some constructions are 'native' and others are 'alien'. The Anglo-Saxons themselves may not have seen things in this way. As in the eighteenth century, so also in the

Anglo-Saxon period, many foreign constructions may to the educated have appeared more natural than the native ones.

The problem of copying is equally important since so few texts survive in the author's autograph. The average medieval reader rarely read a work in the way the author had written it because his copy was one or more removes away from the original. Such readers might have found it difficult to imagine what had been there because their sense of the original was less developed than ours is, trained as we are to recognize printing mistakes. However, even if we today receive a handwritten letter from a friend, part of which is not immediately clear, our inclination is to wonder what he meant by it rather than to jump to the conclusion that he made a writing mistake. Medieval readers no doubt accepted what was in their copy as the text without wondering what may have lain behind it; and this means that they accepted its language.

Let me give a simple example. In Caxton's edition of *Quattuor Sermones* (*c.* 1483) the following sentence occurs: 'And what thou yeuyst gyue hit gladly for the glad yeuer God louyth'.[3] In a manuscript in Trinity College, Cambridge, which contains a somewhat earlier version of this text, though it is not the copy used by the compositor in setting up his edition, the sentence reads: 'and what þat þow yeuest yeue it gladly ffor God louyth the glad yeuere.' We might assume that the Trinity reading represents the original and that Caxton's version is the result of a copying or printing error. Such an assumption may be correct, though it need not be. What is more important in an attempt to evaluate the impact of medieval literature upon its readers is how the medieval reader reacted to Caxton's text. With no knowledge of other versions he presumably assumed that what was in the copy he was reading was acceptable, as indeed we do when only one manuscript of a work survives. If he accepted that 'the glad yeuer God louyth' was an acceptable reading, how did he react to that reading? Would he say that it was different from his spoken language and therefore the written syntax was deliberately perverted for literary ends, or would he accept that in written works the syntax was flexible and individual forms were important only if they were repeated frequently? The likelihood is that he would take the second alternative. If this is so, how much value should we attach to unusual syntactic patterns in medieval literature which may have arisen quite arbitrarily rather than as the result of deliberate literary activity? Although the example I have .chosen is from a prose text, it need not be thought that poetic manuscripts preserved the original text any more accurately. *The Canterbury Tales*, for example, underwent considerable scribal revision.

Closely associated with both translation and copying is the use by an author of an earlier work in English. I have already noted several examples in this book; often a second author took over bodily whole sentences or even longer passages from an earlier one and retained much of the earlier syntax. An example of where an earlier work was used as a major source is Book 5 of Malory's *Le Morte Darthur* which was based on the fourteenth-century alliterative poem *Morte Arthure*. Although the influence of the poem can be traced most easily in Malory's alliterative vocabulary, it extended to a whole range of syntactic usages for in many places Malory imitated or even copied his source. He was not atypical in this. It need not be thought that this type of influence was only from verse to prose, since the prose version of Rolle's *The Form of Living* shows the opposite tendency.[4] There was little to choose between prose and verse linguistically, and the language found in the one was used in the other with little or no modification. The result was that few people could have had any concept of 'natural' syntax in writing, that is a syntax which was consistent in its representation of the language of a man or an area at a given time. Literal translation, copying and the slavish use by authors of earlier English texts all combined to create a mixed syntax in most English writings. Variety in usage, at least in literary texts, was accepted and there was no attempt to produce conformity in syntax. Where there is variety what is exceptional or unusual will appear less remarkable than what is consistent, for the latter will have been consciously created. Our own approach of paying more attention to atypical syntax in a work may not be the most appropriate stance to adopt in reading medieval English literature.

The recognition of this state of affairs has important consequences for our appreciation of medieval English literature. As with word play and other linguistic phenomena it may be that syntactic constructions are significant only when they are accentuated by rhetorical elaboration or repetition of some kind. Deviation by itself is hardly likely to be important. For example, in the opening line of *The Wanderer Oft him anhaga are gebideð* ('Often a solitary man experiences grace') although the order of the second halfline is determined by the alliterative metre, the first three words could be arranged in almost any order since both *anhaga* and *oft* bear the alliterative stave. Would a contemporary audience have reacted differently to any other word order so that we could say that one word order is more significant than another? The answer probably is that a sense of a norm for word order was so little developed in the written language that few readers attached much importance to variations in word order unless the author pointed to the choice he had made. In this case it might be argued that the repetition of *oft* at the beginning of line 8 makes the *oft* here significant. If so, the *oft* gets its emphasis not so much from its position in the clause *vis-à-vis* the subject *anhaga* but from participating in a form of rhetorical repetition extending beyond the sentence.

ORGANIZATION OF LINGUISTIC UNITS

In a short chapter it is not possible to make a comprehensive survey of medieval English syntax; all I can do is to point to certain features of syntax which are different from those in modern English. Let us consider first how a sentence was put together, a point which has been touched on in the chapter on editing. In the medieval period there was no grammatical instruction in the English language, and there were no books in English which corresponded to the Old Icelandic *First Grammatical Treatise* which investigated the Icelandic language of the thirteenth century.[5] Available evidence suggests that interest in English as a language and a means of communication was minimal; what little there was consists of complaint about its wretched condition, though this is merely stated and never analyzed. Grammatical teaching was centred on Latin, or to some extent on French. Naturally, as already noted, there were syntactic patterns in spoken English, but the spoken language was never considered a suitable model to be imitated at the written level. On the contrary, often a written style was praised in relation to the extent it diverged from the spoken norms, for throughout this period there was an attempt to enrich and elaborate English style on the model of Latin and French, and this meant a deliberate turning away from the spoken language. This state of affairs applied as much to prose as to poetry. It was this tendency which discouraged any need for the provision of a grammar of English (for grammars of Latin were readily available) and which allowed rhetoric to take the place of syntax. For rhetoric is concerned with the arrangement of words to produce effects of sound or meaning rather than with the correct syntax of the language or even the logical arrangement of thought. In that respect it may be said that the use of rhetoric and the absence of strict norms of English grammar go hand in hand; when the teaching of grammar became important and influential at the end of the eighteenth century the use of rhetoric in literature went into a decline.

Because it helped to organize language, rhetoric also counteracted the absence of conceptual punctuation in the medieval period. It enabled scribe and reader to follow the organization of a passage just as punctuation and syntax do today, for through it the reader understands the relationship between linguistic units. Even when rhetoric was not involved, the arrangement of the words in a sentence may have been designed to counteract the absence of a conceptual punctuation. In *The Wooing of Our Lord*, for example, we may note the order of *drede* and *with pineful death* in the following sentences:

> Thu biddes me bihalde hu thu faht for me that I poverte of
> worlde ne schome of wicke monnes muth foruten mine gulte ne
> secnesse of mi bodi ne flesches pine drede, hwen that I bihalde
> hu thu was poure for me, hu thu was schent and schomet for
> me, and atte laste with pineful death henged o rode.[6]

Both words appear in an order which seems unnatural. It is possible
to imagine that *drede* was put at the end of its clause in imitation of
Latin, but it is clear that by putting the verb there the whole of the
clause is contained in a readily understandable way. If it had been
put after the 'I', where we might have expected it, the rest of the
clause would have tailed off, and in a manuscript without punctuation it might have been difficult for a reader to determine exactly
how much of what followed should be included with the verb. By
placing the verb at the end, the author made the clause complete
and self-contained. The same could be said of *with pineful death*
which one might expect to follow rather than to precede *henged o
rode*. The order in the manuscript has the virtue that it keeps all the
clause in strict confines, even though we might think that natural
syntax had been flouted in the process.

This may have been a feature of Old English composition as well,
for certainly when this arrangement is included it makes the sense of
the passage much easier to follow. If we consider lines 6–9 of *The
Wanderer* we notice how different each pair of lines is:

> Swa cwæð eardstapa,   earfeþa gemyndig,
> wraþra wælsleahta,   winemæga hryre:
> "Oft ic sceolde ana   uhtna gehwylce
> mine ceare cwiþan."
> (Thus spoke a wanderer mindful of hardships, of dire battles
> through the fall of kinsmen: 'Often in solitude at the break of
> day I had to bewail my cares.')

In the first two lines the verb and subject are in the first halfline:
the rest of the sentence consists of phrasal units which are tacked on.
There is no sense of completeness in the sentence, and if line 7 had
been omitted through copying the sense would hardly be impaired
and there would be no way we could tell of the loss. It is easy to
imagine that a line has been lost after line 7, for there is no way of

saying that the sentence is complete as it stands. This type of construction is found periodically in Old English and produces a kind of
hanging syntax in which certain phrases are left hanging by themselves so that their exact grammatical relationship to the rest of the
sentence is uncertain. In *Daniel* lines 17–18

> oðþæt hie wlenco anwod   æt winþege
> deofoldædum,   druncne geðohtas.
> (until at the banquet pride with evil deeds enveloped them,
> drunken thoughts),

the *druncne geðohtas* can be in apposition to either *hie* ('them') or
wlenco ('pride'), which are respectively the object and the subject,
though the sense is not much affected either way. The use of clichés
which are tacked on at the end of lines or sentences often causes the
same ambiguity. This is not true of *The Wanderer* lines 8–9, for in
this sentence the poet has indicated its confines by putting the
infinitive last, so giving a sense of completeness to the utterance.
All that comes before is part of the clause; and what comes after is
not. It is a feature of this poem that infinitives and some verb forms
are used in this way, which is why lines 6 and 7 are atypical. Another
way of enclosing a clause is by splitting a heavy noun phrase so that
instead of saying 'The king and his ministers went to London' one
would have 'The king went to London and his ministers'. It is not of
course easy to tell whether this or any other arrangement was a
conscious one to indicate the boundaries of a clause, but it is not
improbable. What we might consider normal syntax may have been
distorted by medieval writers for reasons which we today do not find
easy to comprehend because we have other linguistic mechanisms to
achieve those ends. Deviations from a norm may have been adopted
for reasons of intelligibility rather than for stylistic adornment.

It is interesting to speculate to what extent the absence of conceptual punctuation encouraged the retention or even the development of certain types of constructions. A feature of Old English
syntax is the frequency of correlative clauses, in which related
clauses are linked by the same word which may function in different
ways. Thus *þa* (adv. 'then') and *þa* (conj. 'when') or *þær* (adv. 'there')
and *þær* (conj. 'where') are used to join related clauses in a way
which does not happen in Modern English where the conjunction is
used but not the related adverb. In such cases in Old English it is
usual for a particular type of word order to be used in each clause so
that the main clause is distinguished from the adverbial. In the
following passage from *The Anglo-Saxon Chronicle* this arrangement
can be seen:

þa hie þa ealle gegaderode wæron, þa offoron hie þone here
hindan æt Buttingtune . . . þa hie ða fela wucena sæton on twa
healfe þære e . . . þa wæron hie mid metelieste gewægde.[7]
(When they were all assembled, they intercepted the Danes
from the rear at Buttington . . . When they had camped on
both sides of the river for many weeks, they were afflicted with
shortage of provisions.)

Other types of correlation were also found. A pronoun could be used
to anticipate a clause which might otherwise have been in itself the
subject or object. In *The Dream of the Rood* lines 28–9

þæt wæs geara iu,   (ic þæt gyta geman),
þæt ic wæs aheawen   holtes on ende,
(It was a long time ago, I can still recall it, that I was cut down
at the edge of the wood)

the first *þæt* anticipates the *þæt* at the beginning of the next line, for
the clause in line 29 is the real subject of the previous line. The
effect of such correlation on us is one of fussiness and verbosity,
because it is not part of our own linguistic conventions. We may
think authors who use it simple and naive. But constructions like
this played an important role in intelligibility, when punctuation
was not used in the way to which we are familiar. This needs to be
appreciated before critical judgements on style and meaning are
advanced.

In medieval English it was difficult to make up complex sentences
with many subordinate clauses. A glance back to the sentence from
Alfred's preface of the *Cura pastoralis* quoted earlier (p. 138) will
show how difficult he found it to write a complex sentence. It is often
thought that this sentence reveals Alfred's incompetence as a stylist,
but this is an unnecessarily harsh judgement. The clumsiness is
caused by his attempt to impose the structure of one language upon
another language without the linguistic mechanisms to support that
structure. Early English did not have a full range of subordinating
conjunctions. The majority of the conjunctions in Old English had a
co-ordinating function, and even those which could be subordinating,
like *for þæm* and *þær*, were used principally for co-ordination as in
The Wanderer and *The Seafarer*. It is hardly surprising that the
absence of subordinating conjunctions is not noticed more widely,
for there is a tendency to attach greater importance to nouns, adjectives and verbs than to other parts of speech. The words in those
classes belong to what is called the 'open' lexical group, i.e. the
group in which new words can be added indefinitely. Conjunctions,

on the other hand, belong to the 'closed' group. It is rare nowadays for a new conjunction to enter the language, and no doubt many people think of our conjunctions as an unvarying part of the language. They find it difficult to imagine an English in which there were not many subordinating conjunctions, because they are used to lexical innovation and development only within the 'open' group.

The development of subordinating conjunctions is one of the features which distinguishes modern from medieval English. A whole range of these conjunctions was introduced into the language in the late medieval period as a result of borrowing from and imitation of Latin and French. It was the existence of these new conjunctions which made the Ciceronian imitations possible in Elizabethan English; it was their absence in Anglo-Saxon which caused the Alfredian failure. Most other medieval writers accepted the limitations of the language and realized that co-ordination rather than subordination was the most suitable sentence structure in English. There are many examples of this from the very earliest writing in English, such as *The Anglo-Saxon Chronicle*:

> Her hiene bestæl se here on midne winter ofer tuelftan niht to Cippanhamme, ond geridon Wesseaxna lond ond gesæton, ond micel þæs folces ofer sæ adræfdon, ond þæs oþres þone mæstan dæl hie geridon ond him to gecirdon . . .[8]
> (At this point after twelfth night in midwinter the Danish army made its way secretly to Chippenham and overran and occupied all Wessex and drove many of the inhabitants across the sea. The greater part of those left behind were conquered and subjugated.)

It is easy to think that both a style like this and the people who wrote it were simple; but such an assumption is itself too naive. Even in prose texts with a more consciously contrived style than the *Chronicle's*, co-ordination remains the basic principle of construction. An important consequence of this is that certain types of statement are encouraged. Subordination implies qualification, doubt and other factors which temper the pure statement of fact; co-ordination invites bald statement without qualification. This produces a more straightforward, a more blatant, less circumspect and less psychological development of ideas and statements. Furthermore, co-ordinate constructions tend to encourage certain stylistic traits of which repetition, parallelism, balance and contrast are the most important.

Consider the following passage from the *Epistle of Discretion of Stirrings*:

Thou askist me counseil of silence and of speking, of comon dieting and of singuler fasting, of duelling in cumpany and of onely-wonying [living as a solitary] bi thiself. And thou seist that thou art in gret were [doubt] what thou schalt do: for, as thou seist, on the to partie thou art gretly taried with speking, with comyn eting as other folk don and, thou seist, with comyn wonyng in cumpany; and on the tother partie thou dreddist to be streitly [strictly] stille, singuler in fasting and onely in wonyng, for demyng [estimation] of more holynes then thou art worthi and for many other perils. For oftetymes now thees daies thei be demyd for moost holy and fallen into many perils that moost are in silence, in singuler fasting and in onely-duelling.[9]

This passage was written by one of the more admired stylists of the Middle English period, the author of *The Cloud of Unknowing*. At first the passage seems quite complicated, but it is a complication that springs from elaborate parallelism and repetition, not from complex subordination. For there is very little subordination in the passage. From examples like this it is understandable why alliteration with its balanced halflines was the Old English poetic metre, and why Middle English writers took so readily to the couplet, since that is a form of composition which lends itself to statement in each couplet. It is also understandable why so few writers used stanzas and why most who did could not master it, for the stanza demands a large degree of subordination if it is to be used intelligently.

ARTICLES

Between medieval and modern English there are differences in the organization and use of the various parts of speech, some of which have been caused by the fall of inflections from the early Middle English period onwards. One of the most important, if least regarded, is the difference in articles. In modern English it is possible for a word to have no article or to have an article in either the *a* or the *the* form. Since most nouns have a plural and the *a* form is singular only, there are five possible forms in modern English which are illustrated here through the word *boy*:

	Singular	Plural
zero	boy	boys
a	a boy	—
the	the boy	the boys

In practice few nouns exhibit all five forms. Words like *cattle* have only two: 'cattle' and 'the cattle'; and proper names have only one. By and large 'the' indicates a particular individual or thing known to the reader or hearer, whereas 'a' implies an individual person or thing chosen at random from among all those which constitute the total class of the objects in question. When we say 'I bought a book this morning', it is of little importance which particular book it was, but it is significant that it was a book rather than a paper or whatever.

The situation in Old and Middle English is different. In Old English it is often said that there are no articles, though the demonstrative adjective *se, þæt, seo,* from which the Modern English *the* comes, can be used in a way that is not dissimilar from that of the definite article today. Yet in Old English it still has more demonstrative force than *the* does today, though the demonstratives in both Old and Middle English were weaker than ours. When Chaucer writes 'thise riotours thre' (VI. 661) he is using *these* almost like an article.[10] In Old English an important feature in the use of the demonstrative adjective is that it is always followed by the weak form of the adjective; the strong adjectival form is always used when no demonstrative is present. Structurally there must have been a difference between forms with and forms without the demonstrative adjective, even though the reasons for this difference have not been satisfactorily explained. As compared with modern English, Old English has a zero-form article and what might be called a strong demonstrative article. The difficulty is deciding how they responded to those norms and how we should transliterate their linguistic system into our own. In modern English literature there is a tendency to use definite articles frequently, since particularly in poetry there is a feeling that poets are writing for a small circle who will be familiar with the private references suggested by the definite article. Eliot in his *The Waste Land* uses 'the' not only in the title, but also in such expressions as 'the hyacinth girl' though the girl has not been introduced earlier. She is a definite individual only to those who know the frame of reference of the poem.[11] Modern poets use the definite article frequently because it helps to build up a sense of concreteness and particularity. It may be that we extend this idea backwards in time and assume that all poetry deals with concrete events and people.

In the Old English poem *The Wanderer* there are several examples of how a desire to make a poem more concrete can affect our understanding of the poem and our translation of the words without articles. We may note first that the poem is today called *'The' Wanderer*, though it has no title in the manuscript. It could with equal plausibility be called *A Wanderer*. Even before a reader begins to read the poem, modern editors suggest to him that the poem is about one particular individual. This naturally influences the way he approaches some of the words in the poem. Words or phrases used to describe the wanderer, assuming that the poem deals with only one protagonist, are all without article or demonstrative in Old English: *anhaga* (1), *eardstapa* (6), *snottor on mode* (111). In modern English translations it is usual to employ 'the' before these words. However, in the middle of the poem, in that section which is often referred to as gnomic, the expressions *wer* (64), *wita* (65), *beorn* (70), and *gleaw hæle* (73) which are also without article in Old English are more often than not translated into modern English with 'a'. There is nothing in the grammatical framework of Anglo-Saxon to suggest that contemporary readers distinguished these groups in this way. If we consider the lines:

> Swa cwæð eardstapa, earfeþa gemyndig,
> wraþra wælsleahta, winemæga hryre (6–7),
> (Thus spoke a wanderer mindful of hardships, of dire battles through the fall of kinsmen.)

we assume that the poet has one particular man in mind, partly because he makes a speech and partly because he is endowed with certain characteristics. Neither reason is convincing. The *beorn* of line 70 has several attributes recorded in the poem, and 'the one' of line 88, who is generally regarded as an abstraction rather than a real person, makes a speech. In line 6 there is little justification to translate *eardstapa* as 'the wanderer' rather than as 'a wanderer'. The poet may have intended to refer to a type rather than to an individual, and the language he uses supports this view. Certainly the poet did not have recourse to the demonstrative *se* when referring to the *eardstapa*, though if he is the same person as the *anhaga* of line 1 this usage is what one might have expected. Where, as here, there is a different structure in the language from that found today, it is uncertain how we should transfer their structure into our own. It may be that Anglo-Saxons distinguished less readily between individuals and members of a group. Consequently in poems like *The Wanderer* in Old English it is safer to interpret all the article-less nouns as 'a' and to call the poem *A Wanderer*.

In the Middle English period there was a move towards using articles more along the patterns of Modern English, but even by the end of the medieval period there was neither uniformity nor consistency in usage. Some authors use articles more than others: Chaucer is much more modern than Gower. Whether we should attribute these differences to literary, dialectal, metrical or archaizing tendencies is uncertain. The variety makes Middle English unlike both Old and Modern English so that the deductions about usage that one might make for either of these periods is unlikely to be applicable to the intervening one.

VERBS

Medieval English has a limited number of verb tenses. To all intents and purposes there were only two, the present and the preterite. Although a subjunctive mood existed in Old English and even later, the forms in most verbs soon became confused with those of the indicative so that a clear distinction between the two moods was lost. There were likewise few compound tenses in medieval English, for what have become auxiliaries in Modern English had the status at that time of independent verbs with fully developed meanings of their own. This is why Alfred's use of *sceolde* in his translation from *Boethius* quoted earlier (p. 138) is so clumsy, because he was trying to use it as though it were a true auxiliary instead of an independent verb. His use of this form shows the need felt by translators for an auxiliary and the difficulty they had in supplying that need. In the Middle English period verb forms like *can* and *gan* were used in the way that Alfred used *sceolde*, although they too seem unsatisfactory and tautologous. There were a few embryonic compound tenses formed with parts of the verb 'to be' or 'to have' and a participle, but as the participle was declined like an adjective the development of a full compound was not complete. In Middle English these compound forms became more frequent, but they were still few in comparison with the number of total verb forms and they rarely had a separate function from that of the simple preterite. When we consider how extensive compound tenses are in modern English we realize how comparatively poor medieval English was in this respect. Consider, for example, the following modern English forms: I come, I am coming, I do come, I will come, I should come, I would come, I will have come, I should have come, I would have come, etc. The majority of these tenses were expressed by the present or the preterite in medieval English, which is another way of saying that the many nuances of expression in verb forms to which we are accustomed were not attainable in medieval English. The effects that a modern writer like Henry James can achieve through the use of different verb forms were impossible in medieval English.[12] Finally, apart from one or two rare verbs like *hatan* in Old English no verbs had a passive voice, so that if a passive sense was wanted it had to be expressed through some circumlocution such as *man* followed by an active tense. This circumlocution merely increased the number of simple present and preterite forms.

The effect of this paucity of verb tenses and verb forms was considerable. It is said, for example, that Voltaire relied heavily on auxiliary verbs, for his interest lay 'in the relationships between actions and even in motives, rather than in the crude actions themselves'.[13] To develop a technique like that was hardly possible for the medieval English writer. The creation of a psychological story was inhibited by the lack of variety in the verbs. Both Latin and French, the prestige languages in English, had a more developed verb system with numerous tenses in both indicative and subjunctive moods, as well as a number of other devices like the use of participles to extend the verbal system. English authors were familiar with these languages with their more elaborate verbal systems, even if they were not aware exactly how those languages differed from their own. Modern scholars often comment how English translators produce a more simple and straightforward story. The psychology of the French romances, such as those by Chrestien de Troyes, is lost in the English translation which retains the husk of the story but not the kernel of sentiment.

It has been claimed that Englishmen are more practical, less sophisticated and less interested in psychological motivation than the French. This seems improbable, and the reason for the difference between English and French versions of a story may lie in the different languages, particularly in the range of verb forms. Even Chaucer found it difficult to present convincing psychological portraits of character in *Troilus and Criseyde*, perhaps the closest one could get in English to the subtlety of French. The use of simple tenses encouraged statements of fact which could be used as part of contrasts or comparisons to create some tension and psychological effect. Their use detracted from the development of probability, suggestiveness and various degrees of doubt, all of which might be considered desiderata in a long story, particularly one dealing with love and the emotions. This may be one reason why so many of the longer romances in English seem so interminable, because they are not able to present the psychological examination needed to keep a story of that length alive. Simple tenses encourage gnomic and proverbial utterances which embody universal truths rather than specific comments on the situation in hand. They encourage narrative and straight description rather than protracted examination of the various strands of a situation or of the mental state of the participants. In general then the verb system in Old and Middle English made composition that much more difficult for an author in that his writing was less varied and more uniform and in that it demanded the adoption of unusual effects to try and vary the pace, tone and stress of his work. Some writers did not try, which is one reason why many works at that time have a sameness of tone and approach.

Let us look at some pieces from Old and Middle English to see the results of the limitations imposed by the verb system. In an Old English poem like *The Seafarer* (a poem of 124 lines) almost all the verbs are either simple preterite or present ones. There are a few auxiliary verbs, though as we have seen these have the status and force of independent verbs. Among them are *mæg* (1, 94, 100), *meahte* (26), *sceolde* (30) and *wille* (43, 97, 99). In addition there are a few compounds verb forms. Some of these are composed of a part of the verb 'to be' and the past participle, but as this latter is declined like an adjective the verb has hardly developed into a full compound tense. Examples include: *geþrungen wæron* (8–9). There is also one form with *hæbbe* and the past participle (4) and one of *ah* followed by the past participle (27). All the other verbs are either in the present or the preterite, though some of these are in the subjunctive mood. Naturally, therefore, for long stretches in the poem there are passages with only present or preterite verbs with the result that there is a considerable amount of plain statement and description. There is no discussion of the experiences of the seafarer in any particular way; his life is illuminated only as part of the general truths which dominate the life of man and which are stated categorically in the present tense. The result is characteristic of Old English in the poetry of which a description of an event is placed next to a general moral statement, and it is understood that the latter is a comment upon the former though there is nothing except the juxtaposition of the items to indicate this.

Deonise Hid Diuinite, by the author of *The Cloud of Unknowing*, is a translation from Latin, and below are given a passage from it and the Latin original:

It behouiþ us alle þat ben practisers of þis deuinite for to make oure deniinges on þe contrary maner to oure afferminges; for whi we settyng oure affermynges begynnen at þe moost worþi þinges of þees beyng þinges, & so forþe by þe menes we descende to þe leest, bot in oure deniinges we begynnyn at þe leest, & stien up to þe moste, and eftsones by þe menes, from þe hiest to þe last, & fro þe last to þe hiest aȝein, we foulden alle togeders & done hem awey, þat we mowen cleerliche knowe þat vnknowyng, þe whiche is wallid aboute from al knowable miȝtes in alle þees being þinges.

Oportet autem, sicut arbitror, ablationes laudare contrarie quam positiones. Etenim illas a primis incipientes, et per media et ultima descendentes, ponebamus. Hic autem ab ultimis ad principaliora ascensus facientes, et per media rursus ad extrema,

omnia auferimus, ut revelate cognoscamus illam ignorantiam ab
omnibus noscibilibus in omnibus exsistentibus circumvelatam,
et supersubstantialem illam videamus caliginem ab omni lumine
in exsistentibus occultatam.[14]

The Latin is complicated and the English translator has responded
by expanding the passage in an arrangement of parallel clauses. The
Latin was more succinct. More importantly the Latin has an ordered
and consistent use of tenses which is lost by the English translator.
In the first sentence the Latin author uses two participles and an
imperfect tense. The translator reacted by using a present participle
for the imperfect (a tense not represented in English and which
could not be easily translated) and two verbs in the present tense.
In the next sentence the Latin participles are again transformed into
the present tense, but the perfect is rendered by a preterite. The two
subjunctives of the purpose clause are represented by *mowen* and the
infinitive. It need not be denied that this is a good translation in
many ways, though much of the Latin is lost. The ordered progression indicated by the verb forms in the Latin is transformed into a
different kind of parallelism by clauses. The expansion and simpli-
fication of meaning are attributable in part at least to the difference
in the two verb systems. However, in this passage we should remember that the author is translating from Latin, which forces him to
try and develop his verb system to cope with the original.

When translation is not involved, the verb forms are often simpler
and perhaps even less logical in their arrangement. If for example
we look at the opening of *Sir Gawain and the Green Knight*, the siege
of Troy is introduced in the first line in the perfect tense: *watz sesed*.
Then the author uses the preterite (*wroȝt*) to describe the man who
committed treason, though the perfect again (*watz tried*) for his trial.
Afterwards he subjected, in the preterite (*depreced*) kingdoms, though
the other extensions of Trojan influence are mentioned in the present
tense (*ricchis*, *biges* etc.). Although Brutus occupies England in the
present tense, since his time many changes have taken place in the
perfect (*hatz wont*, *hatz skyfted*). Modern English renderings of the
poem usually rearrange these verb forms in a more coherent order,
for it is difficult to see any rational progression of the tenses in the
poem itself. There was a gradual extension of verb forms in Middle
English, but a sifting out and ordering of their meaning came only
later. Variety of form precedes variety of meaning.

The uncertainty about the use of tenses is part of that wider lack
of regulation in the medieval language as a whole. There are many
examples of the lack of concord between subject and verb, as well as
of changes from singular to plural in a list of verbal phrases with the

same subject. There are cases where a subordinate clause has no main clause, as in an earlier chapter. There are many examples of nouns and verbs being declined in an irregular way under the influence of the analogy of other forms, a variety which persisted well beyond the medieval period. It is also quite common to find omission of pronouns, verbs or nouns in a sentence. Some of these features may have arisen accidentally through copying rather than deliberately, but clearly the average reader and writer did not have any real sense of acceptable syntax. How could he when English was subject to so many contrary influences? One result, of course, was that syntax could not be manipulated so easily for stylistic or other ends. Today it is common enough for an author to produce an elliptical style to suggest informality of speech. Thus the use of abbreviated forms like *it's* or the omission of the subject or predicate will indicate a colloquial speech level. This was not possible in medieval English.

In the same way syntax could not be used to create tension in poetry. Today, for example, a poet may strive to let the stress pattern of his metre have a different rhythm from that of normal syntax and this will cause a tension between the two. To do this the syntax needs to be sufficiently regular so that departures from it can be meaningful. As it happens the alliterative metre was then so free that it too would have prevented this tension from being developed. Finally we may note that the absence of accepted syntactic patterns prevented the development of vocabulary in the way to which we are accustomed. The regularizing of the adjective-noun order means that we can distinguish clearly between a *football special* and a *special football*. In Middle English a distinction like this would not have been apparent. It was common then on account of the influence of French to place the adjective(s) after the noun; there was no difference in meaning between *siege perilous* and *perilous siege*. The lack of syntactic regularity would have prevented the extension of meaning in other ways as well, and it may be that this was an important influence in the stereotyping of the vocabulary.

9

Levels of Discourse

THE COLLOQUIAL LEVEL

While scholars accept that there were different levels of language in medieval English literature, no uniform system to describe those differences has emerged. Some use the three levels of style, high, middle and low, recommended by the rhetoricians. Others prefer to talk of a romance style or a historical style. There are frequent references to the language of poetry and the language of prose as though each represents a level of language. Finally, many refer to the colloquial nature of the literary work they are studying as though there is a pronounced difference between the colloquial and literary levels of discourse. It is never made clear, however, if there is any relation among these various styles: whether we should regard the colloquial pieces as written in the low style or whether the language of poetry is equivalent to the high style. Although the historical style is usually considered straightforward, it is not equated with any particular level of discourse. All these systems exist independently of one another; the result is confusion in critical works. So it is appropriate to begin this chapter by considering these concepts.

The colloquial level of language can be represented in two ways, each of which is here illustrated by a quotation. C. S. Lewis, for example, wrote 'The types of classical Old English halflines are, after all, blocks of pure speech rhythm. So are the halflines of the *Brut's* new rhymed (or consonanced, or assonanced) lines.'[1] The use of 'speech rhythm' is met with less commonly now, for 'colloquial' appears to have taken its place. T. H. Bestul writes of the fourteenth-century alliterative *Winner and Waster* 'particularly in the debate proper, the style is most often colloquial'.[2] Common to both approaches is the absence of any definition of what is meant by either speech rhythm or colloquial. At first sight the two ideas appear very different, for there is no proof that Lewis necessarily meant colloquial by his use of 'speech rhythm'. If he did not, it is difficult to decide what he did mean by it unless simply that the work in question is in English. At least Miss Daunt who seems to take rather the same line as Professor Lewis thought that 'old English verse is really the spoken language rather tidied up'.[3] To her there is no difference between Old English poetry and prose, and both are essentially reflections of the rhythm of the spoken language – not only then, but also now. Therefore although those who use 'speech rhythm' in their critical vocabulary may not have colloquial language consciously in mind, that is what they seem to mean. For the feature that links the two together is that the texts which are described as colloquial or with pure English speech rhythm are alliterative ones, as against those which have been influenced by French phrasing, syntax and metre. There is evidently a feeling that French style was literary, artificial and imposed upon a native English speech pattern in a quite arbitrary and unfeeling way. It is only in the alliterative style that the true voice of English emerges.

There are of course many objections to this view, and the grounds for describing a text as colloquial are usually subjective. The principal objections to the whole concept are firstly our ignorance of what the spoken language was like and secondly the essentially literary nature of composition even in the Old English period. There is no way of telling how good a guide the Old and Middle English written texts are to the spoken language of those periods. It is not necessarily correct to assume that the spoken and written levels of language then were closer than they are now. Most attempts to consider the colloquial level of medieval English have concentrated on phonology because it is assumed that the sounds which appear in writing at a given time existed at the colloquial level some time previously.[4] Even if this view is correct, it is no help in deciding what parts of the literary language are colloquial because the same principle is certainly not applicable to other aspects of language. One cannot say that when a new word appears in a written text, it is the emergence of a word in writing that had existed for some time already in speech. The same applies to syntactical usage. Foreign languages exerted too much influence for this to be an acceptable principle to follow in vocabulary or syntax. Although it is possible that some authors did use colloquial words and expressions, the problem has always been to decide which they are.

The results of one attempt to investigate the colloquial nature of Old English vocabulary were tentative, and they suggested it is possible to trace a colloquial influence only in a few words.[5] In the light of our present knowledge we may be able to suggest that the odd word or phrase has a colloquial sense, but there is no possibility of saying that all or even the major part of any text is colloquial. Furthermore it is often assumed that 'colloquial' is equivalent to slang, racy, vulgar, or colourful. There is little evidence to suggest that this is so, and it may be that what appears to us most racy is in fact most literary. Some Middle English lyrics, such as those in Harley 2253, have what appears to be a colloquial base, although most are in fact literary and many are based on foreign models. The colloquial nature of some texts may be something introduced through imitation of foreign texts (the example of Chaucer springs immediately to mind here); it is unlikely to be the result of an English poet listening to the speech of his contemporaries in the market place. We must be cautious of succumbing to romantic ideas of speech and composition.

Literature in the Old English period was as literary as that of any later period, for it cannot have been popular in any meaningful sense. As we have seen in an earlier chapter there was a strong clerical bias to composition. If there was a secular influence, it came from the courts rather than the cottages, though it is difficult to trace any real secular traits in the existing literature except in late Middle English. The influence of Latin was strong and words of Latin origin are found in the poetry. Therefore a distinct non-colloquial element can certainly be discerned in the alliterative style, though this would not of itself mean that colloquial elements were entirely absent. The alliterative style demanded a large number of words with roughly the same meaning because if a line had *b* as its alliterating stave it would, for example, be no use introducing the word *man* in that line. It would be necessary to have a word for 'man' beginning with a *b-*. The solution to this problem was provided by using circumlocutions which were either compounds or phrases of a formulaic nature, or by retaining words which seem otherwise to have passed out of regular use. Many words found in the poetry are found rarely, if at all, in prose; and the most reasonable explanation of this is that some of the words were archaic and had been retained by the poets to help them over the exigencies of alliterative composition. The result is that the vocabulary in poetry was to some extent divorced from speech; it was artificial and contrived. It is interesting to remember in this connection how few Scandinavian words are found in Old English literary texts, although they were present in some parts of the country in large numbers. Their absence is itself an indication that speech was not the model imitated by the writers. The presence of Latin as against Scandinavian words in Old English poetry is explained by the status of Latin, which carried literary prestige. No literary cachet attached to Scandinavian which would be known at the colloquial level alone; there was therefore no reason to use Scandinavian words. If, however, Old English literature had consisted of pure speech units, a higher proportion of Scandinavian words would be expected.

What is true of Old English applies equally to Middle English. French added a further foreign influence on vocabulary and style which offered encouragement to authors to turn away from the colloquial to a more learned and esoteric language. Many words and constructions of Latin and French origin are found. The Church continued to exercise a powerful influence over style and language at least till the end of the Middle English period. If alliteration is closer to the speech of the people, Middle English literature can hardly be described as colloquial. Medieval plays, which consist entirely of dialogue, were written in various rhyming metres. Chaucer, who was one of the few medieval English authors who wrote dramatic dialogue, used the alliterative style only for battle scenes and there is no suggestion of any colloquialism. Many alliterative poems are themselves hardly popular in tone or sentiment. *Sir Gawain and the Green Knight* is an extremely courtly and sophisticated poem, even though it is written in the alliterative style. And *Piers Plowman*, the style of which has been described as colloquial,[6] deals with abstruse topics and introduces a multitude of learned words and allusions.

Those who use the concept 'colloquial' rarely define what they mean by it. It appears to be used in a variety of senses, though usually in a vaguely approving manner. Certainly the style of Old and Middle English texts cannot be described as colloquial in the sense in which that word is used in modern linguistic analyses of speech levels.[7] It is possible that the oral-formulaic theory has influenced some to think that alliterative poetry was colloquial, even in Middle English. However 'oral' does not mean 'colloquial', and modern oral poets like those in Yugoslavia make use of a stock of formulae which have no connection with the colloquial level of speech. In Old and Middle English it was rare to present speech as a different form of language from narrative. In Old English the characters in the poetry speak in the same elevated style as that of the surrounding narrative. A speech by Beowulf is not noticeably different in style from a passage of narrative in *Beowulf*. In Middle English there were some developments in the representation of speech, but these were not generally towards a realistic representation. Most authors continued to use the same vocabulary and syntax in speech as elsewhere. The most noteworthy difference is the use of vocabulary of a coarse, potentially slang-type character. Langland and Chaucer both enlivened their dialogue with coarse words and with words that might be described as low. At *Piers Plowman* B. v. 302

'I haue good Ale, gossib', quod she, 'Gloton,
woltow assaye?'

both *gossib* and *gloton* might be thought of as colloquial language or slang because the dialogue in question takes place in an ale-house. But *gossib* or *gossip* is used frequently as a form of address and was common in literary works in this sense. Although it may well have been used colloquially, it also has a literary aura about it.[9] *Gloton*, a word of French origin, occurs commonly as a term of abuse, particularly in texts translated direct from French. For example, Caxton in his *Charles the Great* (1485) has the following sentence spoken by the Emperor Charles to his nephew Roland: 'Ha, evyl gloton, I have wel herde the spoken'.[10] Since the passage is translated directly from the French *Fierabras*, colloquialism cannot be involved.

This and similar examples must make us pause in any acceptance of a colloquial level for many words. It is quite possible that many words like *gloton* which have the appearance of belonging to a slang or colloquial level were never part of colloquial English. They may have been literary terms of abuse copied from French works in which the words were so used and thus they gradually became part of Middle English literary abuse. The traditional nature of medieval composition would ensure the repetition of these words whether they were part of the colloquial language or not. Similarly Chaucer in his *fabliaux* tales used many terms of abuse. The miller in *The Reeve's Tale* addresses Alan in the following way:

"Ye, false harlot," quod the millere, "hast?
A, false traitour! false clerk!" quod he,
"Thow shalt be deed, by Goddes dignitee!" (I. 4268–70)

Here all three words, *harlot*, *traitour* and *clerk*, are of French extraction and the same can be said of many other words of abuse in this tale.[11] As the French *fabliaux* which Chaucer imitated contained dramatic dialogue, it is reasonable to suppose that Chaucer introduced his own dialogue on the pattern found in the French tales he knew. Thus, in *The Nun's Priest's Tale*, when we find the wife using the word *Avoy*, we cannot think that this is an English colloquialism. It is a word found in the French parallels and is put in the mouth of a country woman because it has a colloquial appearance. But that colloquialism springs from its literary origins, not from its basis in English speech. In general much of the 'colloquial' vocabulary in Middle English was based on French rather than being drawn direct from life, a concept which was in itself quite alien to medieval writers.[12]

Chaucer, Langland and Caxton were quite typical of medieval writers in their use of terms like these. The words suggest the characters of the people in question. People who were wicked or

evil, or angry, or vulgar, were given words of abuse and low words
to indicate their moral character. Low vocabulary was a mark of the
wicked and of those who are acting wickedly at a particular point in
time, because they have been temporarily seduced from their normal
upright lives. This vocabulary acts as a contrast to the more elevated
speech of the good characters. When for example in *Havelok the
Dane* (*c.* 1300) Godard, the regent of Denmark, addresses Havelok
in the following way:

> 'Wiltu ben erl?
> Go hom swiþe, fule drit-cherl.' (681–2),

we recognize the appropriateness of the vocabulary to a man who is
so wicked that he is going to usurp the throne and attempt to kill
the rightful heir. Authors, like that of *Havelok*, were not attempting
to provide realistic dialogue or even to suggest that wicked characters were in any sense lower in class or status than good ones. Godard
was after all an earl and the regent. Their speech is an indication of
their moral behaviour and as such is part of the general representation of wickedness in the tale.

The contrast between 'good' and 'bad' speech is found especially
in the medieval play cycles, where the absence of narration makes
the representation of the moral worth of the characters through their
speech more pressing. In the Wakefield Master's *Mactacio Abel*, for
example, Abel speaks in the normal elevated style, whereas Cain
uses a multitude of low words and terms of abuse:

> *Abell* God, as he both may and can,
>   Spede the, brother, and thi man.
> *Cayn* Com kis myne ars! Me list not ban;
>   As welcom standys theroute.
>   Thou shuld haue bide til thou were cald;
>   Com nar, and other drife or hald –
>   And kys the dwillis toute!
>   Go grese thi shepe vnder the toute,
>   For that is the moste lefe.
> *Abell* Broder, ther is none hereaboute
>   That wold the any grefe. (57–67)[13]

The difference between the speech of these two characters is quite
remarkable; and it is a difference which is found also in the speech
of God and Satan, Christ and the Jews, and others. In such cases we
need not suppose that the audience was meant to think in terms of
colloquial language, though some of the words and phrases used may

have been taken from colloquial levels of speech. It would be a little nonsensical to suppose that one character was speaking colloquially and the person whom he was addressing was using formal language. Author and audience would respond to these general speech levels as indications of moral behaviour;[14] and these differences in speech are very gross and lack any kind of linguistic sophistication. Many of the words used as terms of abuse were literary words, and the authors were not interested in the creation of a colloquial style. It might be sensible if 'colloquial' and 'speech rhythm' were abandoned as critical or stylistic terms in future discussions of medieval literature.

It is appropriate at this point to remind ourselves of the linguistic conditions in England of the Middle Ages, with no standard language and no radio or television to disseminate standard colloquialisms. Thus colloquial words were dialect words which were perhaps unfamiliar in other parts of the country. Are we to assume, for instance, that the supposed colloquialisms in *Piers Plowman* represent the London or the West Midlands dialect? Or shall we accept that there was a national level of colloquialisms? Although certain words like *arse* may have been recognized as vulgar throughout the country, it is probable that the use of words like this in literature gave them their vulgar colouring on a wider scale. Its status as a coarse word probably arose precisely because it was put into the mouths of such people as the devil. This view means of course that there may have been a literary type of vulgar speech which writers would draw upon and which was quite separate from any dialectal level of colloquialism.

Loose syntax, which is thought by many to be the hallmark of alliterative poetry, particularly in Middle English times, is often taken to be another aspect of the colloquial level of some writers. Looseness in syntax is a fluid concept and depends to some extent on how modern scholars edit their texts. Many fifteenth-century prose writers like Caxton are accused of writing rambling and unstructured sentences.[15] Yet since they were imitating or translating French works there can be no question of their using a colloquial style. Looseness is not necessarily a synonym for colloquial, although in the Middle English period alliteration might have seemed formless to some because it lacked the constraints of syllabic counting of the couplet and stanza forms of metre. In Old English the alliterative poets composed by clause and phrase rather than by sentence as we might do; and the Middle English poets were the inheritors of this tradition. This method of composition, which may result in what seems like looseness to us, was a literary method rather than a colloquial style, for there is after all no evidence that looseness of syntax is a reflection of speech. We would not assume it to be so of later writers like Sir Thomas Browne or Laurence Sterne, and there is no reason why we should think it true of the medieval writers.

THE LANGUAGE OF POETRY AND PROSE

Let us turn now to consider the relationship between poetry and prose and the question of whether there were different poetic languages. Although differences in the levels of vocabulary may have existed in Old and Middle English, it is no longer possible for us to trace them for there is no work in English equivalent to the poem *Alvíssmál* in Old Norse. In this poem the god Thor puts various questions to the dwarf Alvíss in a truly gnomic fashion. The questions all concern words or linguistic expressions used by different beings such as the gods, the giants and men. It appears from the poem that there is a basic distinction between the language of men and that of the non-human beings. The former consists of the common, everyday words, the latter of the more archaic and poetic words and expressions.[16] It is not certain how individual is the attitude to language expressed in this poem; but it gives us some guide to the relative status of Old Norse words. There is nothing in English to give us similar guidance. Differences in status could be of importance since if there was such a distinction in lexical usage it would be reflected in the words used respectively in poetry and prose.

As we noted in an earlier chapter, the words 'poetry' and 'prose' are not found in English till the fourteenth century, although there were exceptional cases in which the Latin equivalents were used in early English. The Old English translation of Boethius' *De consolatione philosophiae*, which was written in Latin in alternately metre and prose, contains various sections introduced by the respective words *prosa* and *metrum* as in the Latin. While the absence of distinctive words for poetry and prose in Old and Middle English need not mean that contemporaries failed to distinguish these two, it does at least suggest that they did not make as sharp a division between them as we do. Descriptions of the art of composition, for example, refer to the creative activity in general rather than to poetry or prose in particular. In *Beowulf* when the Danes wish to celebrate Beowulf's killing of Grendel we today understand that a poem was composed, though there is nothing in the words to indicate that it was a poem rather than a prose narrative.

> Hwilum cyninges þegn,
> guma gilphlæden,   gidda gemyndig,
> se ðe ealfela   ealdgesegena
> worn gemunde,   word oþer fand

soðe gebunden;   secg eft ongan
sið Beowulfes   snyttrum styrian
ond on sped wrecan   spel gerade,
wordum wrixlan. (867–74).

(At times the king's retainer, a warrior filled with eloquence and
mindful of traditional stories who could recall any number of
ancient lays, composed new tales truly linked together. Afterwards the man began to weave a tale about Beowulf's exploit
expertly and he told a well-wrought story successfully and he
varied his words.)

As we assume a poem was composed, most modern commentators
understand *soðe gebunden* to mean 'correctly linked in metre'. It
means no more than 'correctly linked', a term which is vague enough
to apply to most forms of composition. One could as easily say that
alliterative prose was *soðe gebunden*. The same might also be said to
apply to the phrase 'With lel letteres loken' in *Sir Gawain and the
Green Knight* (35). We should not forget that in Old English manuscripts poems were generally written in prose form. This may have
been a method they adopted to save valuable vellum, though it
would produce uncertainty in the minds of the readers whether the
individual piece they were reading was prose or poetry. This would
be accentuated in those manuscripts where poetic and prose pieces
are intermingled. This difficulty arises in part because alliterative
verse is neither syllabic nor rhyming. The poetry consists of phrasal
units which are linked together through alliteration of the stressed
words. As similar phrasal units can occur as much in prose as in
poetry, it only needs a prose writer to link his phrases together by
alliteration for him to write what appears to be poetry.[17] It is for
this reason that Miss Daunt and others assume that Old English
poetry consists of pure speech rhythm and that there is no difference
between the rhythm of poetry and that of prose. While we may
accept that the rhythms in prose and poetry are identical, we do not
have to assume that they are necessarily those of speech.

  The question arises whether in Old English literature there is any
difference between those works we print as poetry and those as prose.
All extant Old English poetry is alliterative; much, but by no means
all, of the prose is also alliterative. By itself alliteration does not
constitute a distinguishing feature; one cannot say that because a
work is alliterative it is therefore poetic. The vocabulary, on the
other hand, may provide this distinction. There are, for example,
words found almost exclusively in prose and others found only in
poetry – or at least in what may be called 'strict' poetry, that which
regularly preserves the most common alliterative patterns. Even this

so-called 'strict' poetry contains 'prosaic' words.[18] That certain words are found only in poetry and others only in prose suggests that the Anglo-Saxons distinguished classes or types of words. This division was not rigid. It is doubtful whether poet or audience would have regarded the introduction of a 'prosaic' word in a 'poetic' text as significant; it is, for example, unlikely to have caused shock because it breached the proper decorum. Evidently what we regard as 'strict' poetry was distinguished from other forms of composition by its use of a consciously elevated style with a high concentration of poetic-type words like compounds and archaisms. The dictates of the insistent alliteration in this poetry may have demanded the use of this type of vocabulary. In general, then, an Old English text is likely to have made its literary impact through the overall tone of its vocabulary rather than through the choice of individual words, and through the association of that vocabulary with a high degree of variation and rhetorical elaboration. This would mean that contemporaries did not think of literary works as either poetry or prose, but distinguished them by their level of ornateness which extended in an unbroken chain from the very plain to the highly elaborate. In the Old English period 'strict' 'poetry' was very ornate and some 'prose' was very plain so that at each extreme the level of ornateness corresponded with our own division into poetry and prose. But our division fails to account for that large body of literature which lies between the extremes and it suggests a sharper differentiation than in fact existed. In the Middle English period the situation is different because the vocabulary of alliterative poetry and prose has come closer together. The absence of compounds and the heavy use of foreign words are characteristic of both.

The same stylistic narrowing is found between prose and Middle English rhyming poetry. With the introduction of rhyme and syllabic metres, the difference between poetry and prose became quite clear. This is, however, a difference in form; in vocabulary the two moved closer together, partly because the compounds and archaisms of the older poetry were discarded and partly because both poets and prose-writers borrowed extensively from French. The desire to write ornately was no longer in itself a spur to poetic composition. In Old English literature a desire to write with greater emphasis and decoration led to the use of a more insistent alliteration, which in its turn produced a more 'poetic' vocabulary and rhetorical elaboration. With so little formal difference between poetry and prose, any attempt to write ornately would have resulted in the writing of what we label poetry. In Middle English the formal difference which had sprung up between the two forms meant that writers who wished to write ornately had first to decide whether to use poetry or prose, for this decision did not inevitably lead to poetry as it had done earlier. There is nothing to distinguish the vocabulary of poetry and prose at this time. Long French words which we might consider technical and prosaic were as likely to occur in poetry as in prose, for the longer the words the more elegant the language. There was, furthermore, a steady trickle of texts being turned from poetry into prose and vice-versa – a concept quite alien to Old English methods of composition. In such translations the vocabulary was much the same in both forms except that if anything the vocabulary in poetry was simpler and more stereotyped. A difference in syntax has been noted in that prose prefers doublets and greater subordination whereas poetry uses more inversion and parallelism.[19] This difference should not be pushed too far. In general in the medieval period writers were more concerned with the level of ornateness in their work than with whether it was poetry or prose. The formal differences which sprang up did not immediately force them to use different styles for each.

ORNATE ELOQUENCE
The implication of the evidence presented so far is that the many levels of style which we choose to find in medieval literature such as colloquialism versus literary language or poetic versus prosaic language are better discarded in favour of a literary language measured in terms of ornateness. Each level of ornateness was equally artificial: low style was as much a literary language with a consciously achieved effect as high style. To us it may seem that the upper end of the stylistic range was the artificial one, partly because it is so much more obviously literary with its learned and foreign words and partly because it is the elevated style which comes in for most criticism. It is the style people adopted who wanted to appear better or of a higher status than they were, and so naturally it was criticized in the mouths of those who could not handle it elegantly, for no one would consciously adopt the low style in preference to another. It was particularly at the end of the fourteenth century that attacks on over-elaboration of style commenced.

Playwrights and narrative poets naturally saw in the over-ornate style a means of concentrating on the extravagances of language. It need not follow that people did speak in the way criticized, for such elaboration was a literary joke. The major form of elaboration picked on for comment was the use of Latin and French words. For example the first shepherd says to the third one in the fifteenth-century Wakefield *Prima Pastorum*

> Yee speke all by clergé
> I here by youre clause (240–1),

because he had used the words *restorité* and *appeté*. The sense of *by clergé* is no doubt 'learnedly, like a priest' and would imply the use of a Latinate vocabulary. This does not prevent this same shepherd from quoting Vergil at a later point in the play, for which he is in his turn criticized by the second shepherd, who says 'Tell vs no clergé' (389). These details suggest that the author was not yet able or willing to construct a comic character who spoke in a consistent way which was ridiculed, as Shakespeare was to do with Malvolio or Holofernes. The attack on elevated speech was more in the nature of an easy laugh which was introduced here and there without regard for characterization, for one character could attack the practice one moment and use it the next. This is true in *Mankind* (c. 1465–70) in which New Guise laughs at Mercy for rhyming *denomynacyon* and *communycacyon* by saying 'Ey, ey! yowr body ys full of Englysch Laten' (124), even though New Guise also uses Latinisms.

Attacks on French-based eloquence appear in Chaucer as well as in the plays. Such attacks are included haphazardly even by Chaucer; they do not constitute a consistent criticism of a character's language. Chaucer's Prioress spoke the French of Stratford-atte-Bowe, though there are no French expressions in her speech. On the other hand, the friar of *The Summoner's Tale* uses French phrases, even though this is not commented on either adversely or otherwise by the narrator. Possibly when the friar used the phrases *je vou dy* and *je vous dy sanz doute* (III. 1832, 1938), Chaucer may have wished to suggest his honeyed flattery for which French would be a suitable medium. However, as the author makes no comment and as many speakers at this time almost certainly used French phrases in their speech, it is easy to read too much into them. Herod in the Wakefield *Magnus Herodes* does make some reference to his use of French when at the end of the play he says 'I can no more Franch'. While this could mean simply 'I have nothing further to say', it is usually understood to mean something more like 'I have run out of bombastic speech'. In the play itself Herod does occasionally use a French phrase and it is possible that his use of such phrases was meant to illuminate his vain and proud character, though as a king French was not unsuitable on his lips. If a comment on bombastic speech is implied, it underlines how the joke against French was becoming a stock one introduced without regard to character. For Herod in general speaks the typical language of the villain; he uses vulgarisms, expletives and low words, to which the Primus Consultus refers when he complains of 'all sich langage'. (247).

These examples show that writers in the fourteenth and fifteenth centuries were becoming more conscious of language and its varieties. At first this consciousness was expressed by attacks on inflated expressions, which means the too liberal use of Latin and French, though the import of such words continued unabated. If there is any picture which emerges it is not that Latin and French words were wrong in themselves, but merely that they were inappropriate in the mouths of the lower classes and those who through their faults were reduced to vulgar levels of speech. It is possible that Chaucer's influence may have accelerated the spread of a new attitude to language in that he imported from French a much livelier and apparently realistic level of speech representation through the use of dialect in *The Reeve's Tale* and vulgarisms in his *fabliaux* and for the Host. Even though it is unlikely that when he says of such low speakers that he reflects 'hir wordes proprely' (I. 729) he meant he attempted to represent colloquial speech, nevertheless the greater use of such vulgarisms would ultimately lead to a wider range of speech representation as in the dialect speeches in sixteenth-century literature. Although Chaucer was doing the same thing as many other Middle English writers, his prestige helped the spread of new attitudes to language.

10

Conclusion

This book has necessarily been selective in the matters it has treated and so its conclusions can be only of a general nature. Perhaps the most important one concerns our modern attitude towards medieval English and how it should be taught. Up till the Second World War it was usual, at least in England, to teach Old and Middle English literary texts as though they were simply philological documents, and the texts were studied through the important cruces they contained. Relatively little attention was directed to the overall structure and meaning of the works. With the growth of critical studies in modern English literature, often under the slogan of reading literature as literature, teachers of medieval literature have increasingly directed their students' attention to the literary excellencies of their texts. In this process the language has been relegated to a position of unimportance as if it were simply a necessary evil to be got out of the way as quickly as possible before the interesting parts of the course commenced.

There is no doubt that this process has gone too far, for it is now possible for undergraduates to talk about the 'meaning' of their texts without understanding the language of those texts. While it may not be necessary for them to have such a wide knowledge of Old and Middle English phonology as was customary, it remains essential for them to have some familiarity with the structure of the early language and the linguistic conditions in which it flourished. Paradoxically more recent scholarship has shown a growing interest in style, though without a grounding in the language behind them modern studies must remain somewhat suspect. The absence of a linguistic base to much modern scholarship has resulted in successive waves of critical approaches washing over early English literature as though each new theory contained the solution to explain its difficulties. Most of these theories were developed for modern literature or for the study of other medieval vernaculars, and they have been applied to medieval English literature without regard to their suitability to match the linguistic conditions of that time and place. This is hardly surprising since criticism is now considered so much more important than language. Nevertheless, I hope this book has shown how central to any literary appreciation is a knowledge of the language. It may be that we need to revise the way in which the language is taught so that greater emphasis is paid to vocabulary and syntax than to phonology. Furthermore, familiarity with the structure of modern, as well as medieval, English helps to highlight the differences between the two and so prevents the easy assumption that whatever is done now could be done then. The language is, as it always has been, the foundation for all studies in literature; it is the rock on which many critical bubbles burst.

In comparison with modern English the two important aspects of medieval English are a lack of tradition and a lack of precision, both of which were caused by the absence of formal instruction in the language. Without such instruction there was no standardization of grammatical forms, punctuation lacked precision, and words remained less clearly defined than now. The lack of tradition meant that words could not acquire the connotative force through literary reference and so they remained as vague stylistic counters instead of carrying localized associations and meaning. The precision which our modern punctuation and word-order make possible encourages us to strive for clarity in expression. We assume that the same is true in the medieval period. With our education in English, we accept that our language is a sufficient medium of literary composition with many strengths. In this development tradition is an important element. It might be said that today writers in English exploit the language's own resources, whereas in the medieval period they exploited those of French and Latin in their attempt to extend the range of English. The result was that style became more general and decorative than we like and that expression fell into stereotyped patterns. There are advantages in and pleasures to be gained from language used in this way, but they are not identical with those in modern English. Criticism which pretends they are can only mislead.

Some may think that Chaucer is the one writer who stands outside the general run of medieval writing in English and who can be appreciated in a more modern way. This is a deceptive attitude, for no one can stand outside his linguistic environment. It is true, nevertheless, that Chaucer is different from many of his contemporaries, particularly in his acquaintance with foreign literature. His knowledge of French and Italian provided him with that sense of tradition which English could not and which his contemporaries lacked. He therefore appreciated more clearly than many the strengths and weaknesses of English as a medium of composition and what constraints the linguistic situation imposed upon anyone who sought to extend its possibilities. His reaction was the same in essence, if not in quality, as that of most other writers in English. He attempted to introduce French linguistic habits into English and he extended the application of those features of language traditionally used by English authors. In the portrait of the Prioress in *The General Prologue* it has been shown that he used words typical of descriptions of noble ladies in French.[1] If this portrait is ironic it is because it has borrowed the French idiom rather than built upon an English one. Those with no French could easily misunderstand the import of the description. Even here, however, it is not the individual word which is significant, as would be true in modern literature, so much as the combination of such words typically used in portrayal of noble ladies. The words are meaningful only within the larger pattern. On the other hand in his article 'Idiom of Popular Poetry in The Miller's Tale' Professor Donaldson shows how Chaucer makes use of certain words for particular effects.[2] It could be argued that here Chaucer was acting as a modern and injecting into his vocabulary more connotation than I have suggested in this book was possible in the medieval period. I do not think this would be the correct interpretation. What takes place in this tale is that words of one stylistic level, the elevated courtly love style, are used in a situation in which a lower stylistic level would be more appropriate because the characters are not of sufficient standing to use the elevated style. The result is the typical burlesque situation of inappropriateness. This is found in many writers in medieval English, though it may be argued that Chaucer exploits it with more finesse. Individually the words would not attract much comment. They are made to do so either through repetition, as in the case of *hende*, or through being linked together with other words from the same elevated stylistic level. The result is cumulative rather than individual.

An understanding of stylistic manipulation in the medieval period enables us to appreciate the effects that authors were aiming at, and this applies as much to Chaucer as to others. *The Pardoner's Tale* provides an example of how we may neglect this in favour of modern concerns for psychology and characterization. The Pardoner introduces his tale in a way that reveals the tricks of his trade; this introduction is delivered in a relatively plain style. As soon as he begins his tale, which is prefaced by a long homily on the vice of avarice, the Pardoner raises his language to the high style. The style of the tale, when compared with the style of the introduction, can be understood only as an assumed style which he adopts professionally when he wants to impress and overawe his listeners. To that extent the contrast between them exhibits the Pardoner's hypocrisy.

After the conclusion of the tale, the Pardoner invites the pilgrims to offer to his relics, but he meets with a rebuke from the Host delivered in the coarsest language. Often we concentrate upon the appropriateness of this language for the Host. A more important consideration is that this low vulgar style is meant as a contrast with the Pardoner's own inflated professional language and it serves as a way of stripping him of his hypocrisy. A man who deceives linguistically deserves to be exposed linguistically: his downfall matches his own pretensions. The Host replies to the Pardoner in the latter's true language, the language of a man who the other pilgrims were afraid would tell a tale of *ribaudye*. The victim is angry because he has been exposed so clearly and so cruelly: no one likes to have his social mask ripped away so uncompromisingly. This effect is achieved through traditional medieval means and it is echoed by the fall of the rioters within the tale itself. The rioters use a low vulgar speech whereas the old man uses a plain style. The old man himself comments on the difference by criticizing their use of the low style to him:

> But, sires, to yow it is no curteisye
> To speken to an old man vileynye,
> But he trespasse in word, or elles in dede. (VI. 739–41)

The rioters are as justly punished for their presumption as the Pardoner is for his. In the tale language styles are important and help to underline the moral which it inculcates. This effect, which is achieved in a traditional manner, is of primary importance in any assessment of the meaning and status of the tale; yet it is frequently ignored.

This last example underlines another important conclusion, namely that investigations into language cannot proceed very far without encountering important critical questions. I would not wish to claim that a study of the language is the only possible approach for medieval literature; but it is an essential one which if it were more considered would prevent many of the extravagances of criticism today. I hope this book has shown how we as moderns have to adjust our linguistic expectations to medieval conditions and how, as we make that adjustment, we raise fundamental problems about the meaning of the texts we are reading. The study of language and literature cannot be divorced, and in the medieval period at least they should be mutually enriching.

Notes

Notes

CHAPTER 1

1. This state has not of course been accepted by all. See for a recent discussion W. S. Howell, *Poetics, Rhetoric, and Logic*, 1975, pp. 17–22.
2. A. C. Spearing, *Criticism and Medieval Literature*, 2nd edn, 1972, ch. 1.
3. See for example L. M. Paterson, *Troubadours and Eloquence*, 1975.
4. G. Kane, 'A Short Essay on the Middle English Secular Lyric', *Neuphilologische Mitteilungen* 73, 1972, p. 112.
5. N. F. Blake, 'Wynkyn de Worde and the *Quatrefoil of Love*', *Archiv* 206, 1969, pp. 189–200; and P. J. Frankis, 'The Syllabic Value of Final "-es" in English Versification about 1500', *Notes and Queries*, 212, 1967, pp. 11–12.
6. These questions are discussed in E. G. Stanley, 'The Use of Bob-lines in *Sir Thopas*', *Neuphilologische Mitteilungen* 73, 1972, pp. 417–26.
7. Cf. C. S. Lewis, 'The Genesis of a Medieval Book', *Studies in Medieval and Renaissance Literature*, 1966, pp. 18–40; and G. Kane, *The Autobiographical Fallacy in Chaucer and Langland Studies*, 1965.
8. Unless otherwise stated Chaucerian poems are quoted from F. N. Robinson, *The Works of Geoffrey Chaucer*, 2nd edn, 1967.
9. N. F. Blake, *Caxton's Own Prose*, 1973, pp. 61–3.
10. N. F. Blake, 'William Caxton: The Man and his Work', Eight Papers Presented to the Caxton International Congress, 1976: *Journal of the Printing Historical Society* 11, 1976–7, pp. 64–80.
11. R. W. Southern, *St. Anselm and his Biographer*, 1963, pp. 17–18.
12. L. F. Powell, *The Mirror of the Blessed Lyf of Jesu Christ*, 1911, p. 165.
13. P. Hodgson, *The Cloud of Unknowing*, EETS o.s. 218, 1944, p. 71.
14. W. F. Bolton, 'The Alfredian Boethius in Ælfric's "Lives of Saints"', *Notes and Queries* 217, 1972, pp. 406–7.
15. A. G. Brodeur, 'A Study of Diction and Style in Three Anglo-Saxon Narrative Poems', in *Nordica et Anglica*, ed. A. H. Orrick, 1968, pp. 100–102. See also L. J. Peters, 'The Relationship of the Old English *Andreas* to *Beowulf*', *PMLA* 66, 1951, pp. 844–63.

16. N. F. Blake, *Caxton and his World*, 1969, pp. 166–7.
17. J. Norton-Smith, *James I of Scotland: The Kingis Quair*, 1971, ll. 211–24.
18. V. J. Scattergood, *The Works of Sir John Clanvowe*, 1975, p. 35.
19. B. J. Whiting, 'A Fifteenth-Century English Chaucerian', *Mediaeval Studies* 7, 1945, p. 40.
20. For other Chaucerian echoes see G. Langenfelt, *Select Studies in Colloquial English of the Late Middle Ages*, 1933, pp. 35–6; and D. Pearsall, 'John Capgrave's *Life of St. Katherine* and Popular Romance Style', *Medievalia et Humanistica* n.s. 6, 1975, pp. 121–37.
21. J. D. Burnley, 'The Morality of *The Merchant's Tale*', *The Yearbook of English Studies* 6, 1976, pp. 16–25.

CHAPTER 2

1. Quotations from Old English poetry are from G. P. Krapp and E. v. K. Dobbie, *The Anglo-Saxon Poetic Records*, 6 vols., 1931–53.
2. The translations of Old English quotations are included as a general aid to the reader whose knowledge of the language may be limited so that he can understand the import of what follows. As the language itself is often under discussion, the translations should be regarded as provisional. They are not intended as polished renderings.
3. C. Jones, 'The Grammatical Category of Gender in Early Middle English', *English Studies* 48, 1967, pp. 289–305.
4. C. T. Onions, 'The English Language', in *The Character of England*, ed. Sir Ernest Barker, 1947, p. 286.
5. H. Gneuss, 'The Origin of Standard Old English and Æthelwold's School at Winchester', *Anglo-Saxon England* 1, 1972, pp. 63–83. See also D. G. Scragg, *A History of English Spelling*, 1974, pp. 1–51, for a general history of spelling in the medieval period.
6. See G. L. Brook, 'A Piece of Evidence for the Study of Middle English Spelling', *Neuphilologische Mitteilungen* 73, 1972, pp. 25–8. The passage corresponds to lines 26663ff of Madden's edition.
7. J. H. Blunt, *The Myroure of Oure Ladye*, EETS e.s. 19, 1873, pp. 7–8.
8. N. F. Blake, *Caxton's Own Prose*, 1973, p. 79.
9. Cf. R. F. Jones, *The Triumph of the English Language*, 1953, pp. 3–31.
10. See T. Finkenstaedt, *You und thou: Studien zum Anrede in Englischen*, 1963.
11. M. M. Crow, '*The Reeve's Tale* in the Hands of a North Midland Scribe', *Studies in English (University of Texas)* 18, 1938, pp. 14–24.
12. On the fall in the status of Kentish, see N. F. Blake, 'Born in Kent', *Lore and Language* 2.5, 1976, pp. 5–9.

13. See E. Schultz, *Die englischen Schwankbücher*, 1912.
14. Some Old English was known in Middle English; see A. F. Cameron, 'Middle English in Old English Manuscripts', in *Chaucer and Middle English Studies*, ed. B. Rowland, 1974, pp. 218–29.
15. H. E. Allen, *English Writings of Richard Rolle*, 1931, p. 7.
16. This difficulty which is not mentioned by medieval readers finds eloquent expression in the sixteenth and seventeenth centuries. Thomas Blount in the preface of his *Glossographia* (1656) writes: 'I was often gravelled in English Books; that is, I encountered such words, as I either not at all, or not throughly understood'; and he was acquainted with Greek, Latin and French as well as with other languages.
17. One sixteenth-century example is found in Cambridge University Library MS. Ll. 4. 14 fol. 169b–170b. These glosses are printed in W. W. Skeat, *The Vision of William concerning Piers the Plowman . . . The 'Crowley' Text; or Text B*, EETS 38, 1869, pp. 421–4.
18. Quotations from *Piers Plowman* are, unless otherwise stated, from G. Kane and E. Talbot Donaldson, *Piers Plowman: The B Version*, 1975, though I have not reproduced their square brackets.

CHAPTER 3

1. See E. J. Dobson, *The Origins of Ancrene Wise*, 1976.
2. See M. Görlach, *The Textual Tradition of the South English Legendary*, 1974.
3. M. M. Crow, 'John of Angoulême and his Chaucer Manuscript', in *Studies in Medieval, Renaissance, American Literature: A Festschrift*, ed. B. F. Colquitt, 1971, pp. 33–44.
4. K. Sisam, *Studies in the History of Old English Literature*, 1953, p. 97ff.
5. Naturally not all editors agree on what to italicize. Thus Robinson himself does not italicize 'Graunt mercy' in *The Canon's Yeoman's Tale* VIII. 1156, though some editors such as A. V. C. Schmidt, 1974, do.
6. R. H. Robbins, *Secular Lyrics of the XIVth and XVth Centuries*, 1955, no. 160.
7. Here quoted from J. A. W. Bennett, *Langland: Piers Plowman*, Clarendon Medieval and Tudor Series, 1972, p. 7.
8. P. M. Wetherill, *The Literary Text*, 1974, pp. xii–xiii.
9. A. J. Bliss, 'Single Half-lines in Old English Poetry', *Notes and Queries* 216, 1971, pp. 442–9.
10. M. Swanton, *The Dream of the Rood*, 1970, pp. 94, 126.
11. G. V. Smithers, *Kyng Alisaunder*, 2 vols., EETS o.s. 227, 237, 1952, 1957, I. 36–7.
12. G. Kane and E. Talbot Donaldson, *Piers Plowman: The B Version*, 1975, particularly pp. 128–220.

13. A. V. C. Schmidt, *The General Prologue to the Canterbury Tales and The Canon's Yeoman's Prologue and Tale*, 1974, p. 127.

14. See P. Clemoes, *Liturgical Influence on Punctuation in Late Old English and Early Middle English Manuscripts*, 1952; W. J. Ong, 'Historical Backgrounds of Elizabethan and Jacobean Punctuation Theory', *PMLA* 59, 1944, pp. 349–60; P. Simpson, *Shakespearian Punctuation*, 1911; P. G. Arakelian, 'Punctuation in a Late Middle English Manuscript', *Neuphilologische Mitteilungen* 76, 1975, pp. 614–24.

15 N. F. Blake, *Selections from William Caxton*, Clarendon Medieval and Tudor Series, 1973, pp. 41–2.

16. N. F. Blake, *Caxton: The History of Reynard the Fox*, EETS 263, 1970, p. 103.

17. S. Booth, *An Essay on Shakespeare's Sonnets*, 1969, pp. 149–51.

18. E. Vinaver, *The Works of Sir Thomas Malory*, 1954, p. 761.

19. A. V. C. Schmidt, *ed. cit.* p. 101; the lines correspond to VIII. 922–3.

20. E. Vinaver, *ed. cit.* p. 773.

21. D. S. Brewer, *Malory: The Morte Darthur*, 1968, p. 62.

22. C. E. Wright, *The Cultivation of Saga in Anglo-Saxon England*, 1939.

23. J. A. W. Bennett, *ed. cit.* p. 50. The Kane/Donaldson edition reads *vigilate* with italics but no capitals. In their edition the lines are numbered 442–3.

24. Kane/Donaldson v. 473–6 is identical.

25. N. F. Blake, *Caxton and his World*, 1969, ch. 7.

CHAPTER 4

1. See further N. F. Blake, 'Some Problems of Interpretation and Translation in the OE *Phoenix*', *Anglia* 80, 1962, pp. 50–62.

2. See B. J. Timmer, '*Wyrd* in Anglo-Saxon Prose and Poetry', *Neophilologus* 26, 1941, pp. 24–33, 213–28.

3. H. R. Ellis Davidson, *Gods and Myths of Northern Europe*, 1964, p. 65.

4. J. McKinnell, 'On the Date of *The Battle of Maldon*', *Medium Ævum* 44, 1975, pp. 121–36.

5. A. T. Bödtker, *Partonope of Blois*, EETS e.s. 109, 1912, p. 70.

6. D. S. Brewer, *Chaucer*, 3rd edn, 1973, p. 111.

7. T. F. Simmons and H. E. Nolloth, *The Lay Folks' Catechism*, EETS o.s. 118, 1901, p. 62.

8. N. F. Blake, *Caxton and his World*, 1969, p. 125ff.

9. G. G. Perry, *Religious Pieces in Prose and Verse*, rev. edn, EETS o.s. 26, 1914, p. 47.

10. R. M. Lumiansky and D. Mills, *The Chester Mystery Cycle*, EETS s.s. 3, 1974, p. 19.

11. N. F. Blake, *Caxton: The History of Reynard the Fox*, EETS 263, 1970, p. 74.

12. Cf. R. F. Lawrence, 'The Formulaic Theory and its Application to English Alliterative Poetry', in *Essays on Style and Language*, ed. R. Fowler, 1966, p. 17.

13. C. S. Lewis, *Studies in Medieval and Renaissance Literature*, ed. W. Hooper, 1966, pp. 4–5; and cf. A. J. Bliss, *Sir Orfeo*, 2nd edn, 1966, p. 53; *'dune* is the more obvious reading, but *dim* is certainly more poetic'.

14. Noted in D. S. Brewer, 'Gothic Chaucer', in *Geoffrey Chaucer*, ed. D. S. Brewer, 1974, p. 6.

CHAPTER 5

1. For example, R. Axton, *European Drama of the Early Middle Ages*, 1974, p. 177, in his discussion of the debt of the Towneley *Cain and Abel* play to agricultural folk drama, says of the name of the character Pikeharnes that a 'pun on harneys as sexual parts ('privy harneys') may also be intended'. It is not suggested that this pun has any relevance to the play.

2. J. H. Wilson, *Christian Theology and Old English Poetry*, 1974, p. 116.

3. H. Kökeritz, *Shakespeare's Pronunciation*, 1953, p. 95.

4. Quoted in C. Ricks, *Keats and Embarrassment*, 1974, p. 59.

5. Kökeritz, *op. cit.* p. 87.

6. D. W. Robertson Jr, *A Preface to Chaucer*, 1963, p. 255.

7. As for example P. F. Baum, 'Chaucer's Puns', *PMLA* 71, 1956, pp. 225–46; and B. F. Huppé, *'Petrus id est Christus:* Word Play in *Piers Plowman*, The B-text', *ELH* 17, 1950, pp. 163–90.

8. K. S. Block, *Ludus Coventriae*, EETS e.s. 120, 1922, p. 104.

9. J. Reidy, *Thomas Norton's Ordinal of Alchemy*, EETS 272, 1975, pp. xlii–xliii.

10. J. E. Seaton, *Sir Richard Roos*, 1961. The attempt to find an acrostic in *Ancrene Wisse* by E. J. Dobson in his *The Origins of Ancrene Wisse*, 1976, p. 312ff is equally unconvincing.

11. R. K. Gordon, *Anglo-Saxon Poetry*, rev. edn, 1954, p. 308.

12. R. A. Peck, 'Theme and Number in Chaucer's *Book of the Duchess*', in *Silent Poetry*, ed. A. Fowler, 1970, p. 100; and B. F. Huppé and D. W. Robertson Jr, *Fruyt and Chaf*, 1963, pp. 49–50.

13. Some of these are available in J. J. Murphy, *Three Medieval Rhetorical Arts*, 1971.

14. N. F. Blake, *Middle English Religious Prose*, 1972, p. 61.

15. *ibid.* p. 82.

16. *ibid.* p. 69.

17. N. F. Blake, *Caxton: The History of Reynard the Fox*, EETS 263, 1970, p. 15 (with punctuation added).

18. H. M. R. Murray, *The Middle English Poem, Erthe upon Erthe*, EETS o.s. 141, 1911, p. 1.

19. R. H. Robbins, *Secular Lyrics of the XIVth and XVth Centuries*, 2nd edn, 1955, p. 11.

20. *ibid.* pp. 15–16.

CHAPTER 6

1. J. Peter, *Complaint and Satire in Early English Literature*, 1956, particularly ch. 1.

2. P. Lehmann, *Die Parodie im Mittelalter*, 2nd edn, 1963, p. 3. This book contains a useful discussion of parody in medieval literature.

3. N. Davis, *Non-Cycle Plays and Fragments*, EETS s.s. 1, 1970, p. 90.

4. G. H. Mair, *Wilson's Arte of Rheorique* 1560, 1906, p. 163. Cf. C. Barber, *Early Modern English*, 1976, pp. 82–4.

5. See R. F. Jones, *The Triumph of the English Language*, 1953, p. 68ff.

6. M. Beerbohm, *A Christmas Garland*, 1912, pp. 125–30.

7. R. W. V. Elliott, *Chaucer's English*, 1974, p. 179.

8. As for example M. Schlauch, 'The Art of Chaucer's Prose', in *Chaucer and Chaucerians*, ed. D. S. Brewer, 1966, p. 153ff.

9. D. Palomo, 'What Chaucer really did to *Le Livre de Mellibee*', *Philological Quarterly* 53, 1974, pp. 304–20. Cf. 'The *Melibee* is thus a very subtle stylistic parody, but one that would not be readily apparent to the modern reader' (p. 306).

10. F. N. Robinson, *The Works of Geoffrey Chaucer*, 2nd edn, 1957, p. 521.

11. A. C. and J. E. Spearing, *Poetry of the Age of Chaucer*, 1974, pp. 199–200.

12. R. H. Robbins, *Secular Lyrics of the XIVth and XVth Centuries*, 2nd edn, 1955, p. 221.

13. L. H. Loomis, 'Chaucer and the Auchinleck MS: *Thopas* and *Guy of Warwick*', in *Essays and Studies in Honor of Carleton Brown*, 1940, pp. 111–28.

14. J. Burrow, 'Listeth, Lordes: Sir Thopas 712 and 833', *Notes and Queries* 213, 1968, pp. 326–7.

15. W. H. French and C. B. Hale, *Middle English Metrical Romances*, 1930, p. 992.

16. W. Heuser, *Die Kildare-Gedichte*, 1904, p. 146.

CHAPTER 7

1. N. F. Blake, *Caxton's Own Prose*, 1973, pp. 100–101.

2. J. A. Burrow, *Ricardian Poetry*, 1971, p. 42.

3. R. O. Payne, *The Key of Remembrance*, 1963, p. 188ff.

4. N. F. Blake, *Middle English Religious Prose*, 1972, p. 133.

5. Some editions break up the sense of 'threeness' by the punctuation they use, for it is not uncommon to find a comma rather than a question mark after *mearg*. Most editions put the caesura after *mago* to attempt to provide a regular Old English line. See further chapter 3.

6. The matter is discussed in greater detail by H. Ringbom, *Studies in the Narrative Technique of Beowulf and Lawman's Brut*, 1968, who gives parallel passages from Wace and Laȝamon.

7. N. Jacobs, 'Alliterative Storms: A Topos in Middle English', *Speculum* 47, 1972, pp. 695–719.

CHAPTER 8

1. *Sweet's Anglo-Saxon Reader*, rev. edn D. Whitelock, 1967, p. 14.

2. *ibid.* p. 5.

3. N. F. Blake, *Quattuor Sermones printed by William Caxton*, 1975, p. 45.
4. N. F. Blake, '*The Form of Living* in Prose and Poetry', *Archiv* 211, 1974, pp. 300–308.
5. It may also be noted that there is no English equivalent to the Edda of Snorri Sturlason, which may be an indication that there was no pagan Germanic background in Old English which needed explanation.
6. N. F. Blake, *Middle English Religious Prose*, 1972, p. 67.
7. *Sweet's Anglo-Saxon Reader*, rev. edn D. Whitelock, 1967, p. 37.
8. *ibid.* p. 32.
9. N. F. Blake, *Middle English Religious Prose*, 1972, pp. 119–20; for an analysis of the style of this paragraph see p. 24.
10. N. E. Osselton, 'Chaucer's "clumsy transition" in the Pardoner's Tale', *English Studies* 49, 1968, pp. 36–8.
11. See particularly G. Rostrevor Hamilton, *The Tell-Tale Article*, 1949, for an analysis of the article in modern poetry.
12. I. Watt, 'The First Paragraph of *The Ambassadors*: An Explication', *Essays in Criticism* 10, 1960, pp. 250–74.
13. R. A. Sayce, *Style in French Prose*, 1953, p. 34.
14. P. Hodgson, *Deonise Hid Diuinite*, EETS o.s. 231, 1955, pp. 6–7, 96.

CHAPTER 9

1. *Studies in Medieval and Renaissance Literature*, 1966, pp. 22–3.
2. *Satire and Allegory in Wynnere and Wastoure*, 1974, p. 90.
3. 'Old English Verse and English Speech Rhythm', *Transactions of the Philological Society*, 1946, p. 64.
4. As in F. P. Magoun Jr, 'Colloquial Old and Middle English', *Harvard Studies and Notes in Philology & Literature* 19, 1937, pp. 167–73.
5. B. von Lindheim, 'Traces of Colloquial Speech in OE', *Anglia* 70, 1951, pp. 22–42.
6. *Langland: Piers the Plowman*, translated by J. F. Goodridge, 1959, p. 309: 'It will be noticed that the rhythms and language are very colloquial'.
7. As in D. Crystal and D. Davy, *Investigating English Style*, 1969.
8. See R. A. Waldron, 'Oral-Formulaic Technique and Middle English Alliterative Poetry', *Speculum* 32, 1957, pp. 792–804 and L. D. Benson, *Art and Tradition in Sir Gawain and the Green Knight*, 1965, pp. 110–66.
9. M.E.D. god-sib(be *n.*
10. N. F. Blake, *Selections from William Caxton*, 1973, p. 26.
11. M.E.D. clerk *n.*, harlot *n.*, O.E.D. Traitor *n.*
12. C. S. Lewis, 'The Genesis of a Medieval Book', *Studies in Medieval and Renaissance Literature*, 1966.
13. A. C. Cawley, *The Wakefield Pageants in the Towneley Cycle*, 1958, pp. 2–3. Other quotations from the Wakefield Master are from this edition.

14. On a similar attitude to 'rude behaviour' which was fitting for non-Christians in religious drama; see G. Wickham, *The Medieval Theatre*, 1974, pp. 52–3. On the medieval attitude towards morality in the romances and how it was expressed through themes and language see L. D. Benson, *Malory's Morte Darthur*, 1976.
15. R. R. Aurner, 'Caxton and the English Sentence', *University of Wisconsin Studies in Language and Literature* 18, 1923, pp. 23–59; see also N. F. Blake, *Caxton's Own Prose*, 1973, p. 36ff.
16. L. Moberg, 'The Languages of *Alvíssmál*, *Saga-Book* 18, 1970–3, pp. 299–323.
17. See further N. F. Blake, 'Rhythmical Alliteration', *Modern Philology* 67, 1969–70, pp. 118–24.
18. See E. G. Stanley, 'Studies in the Prosaic Vocabulary of Old English Verse', *Neuphilologische Mitteilungen* 72, 1971, pp. 385–418.
19. N. F. Blake, '*The Form of Living* in Prose and Poetry', *Archiv* 211, 1974, pp. 300–308.

CHAPTER 10
1. J. L. Lowes, 'Simple and Coy', *Anglia* 33, 1910, pp. 440–51.
2. E. Talbot Donaldson, 'Idiom of Popular Poetry in *The Miller's Tale*', in his *Speaking of Chaucer*, 1970, pp. 13–29.

Select Bibliography

Select Bibliography

The following brief list of books is designed to give a representative selection of approaches to medieval style and literature.

E. Auerbach (trans. R. Manheim), *Literary Language and its Public in Late Latin Antiquity and in the Middle Ages*, London, 1965.

A. C. Bartlett, *The Larger Rhetorical Patterns in Anglo-Saxon Poetry*, New York, 1935.

N. F. Blake, 'Caxton and Courtly Style', *Essays and Studies* n.s. 21, 1968, pp. 29–45.

M. Borroff, *Sir Gawain: A Stylistic and Metrical Study*, New Haven and London, 1962.

D. S. Brewer, ed., *Chaucer and Chaucerians. Critical Studies in Middle English Literature*, London, 1966.

A. G. Brodeur, *The Art of Beowulf*, Berkeley and Los Angeles, 1959.

J. A. Burrow, *Ricardian Poetry*, London, 1971.

A. Campbell, 'The Old English Epic Style', in *English and Medieval Studies Presented to J. R. R. Tolkien*, London, 1963, pp. 13–26.

J. J. Campbell, 'Knowledge of Rhetorical Figures in Anglo-Saxon England', *JEGP* 66, 1967, pp. 1–28.

H. J. Chaytor, *From Script to Print: An Introduction to Medieval Vernacular Literature*, Cambridge, 1945.

C. Clark, '*Sir Gawain and the Green Knight*: Characterisation by Syntax', *Essays in Criticism* 16, 1966, pp. 361–74.

D. L. Clark, 'Rhetoric and the Literature of the English Middle Ages', *Quarterly Journal of Speech* 45, 1959, pp. 19–28.

E. R. Curtius (trans. W. R. Trask), *European Literature and the Latin Middle Ages*, New York, 1953.

E. T. Donaldson, *Speaking of Chaucer*, London, 1970.

R. Frank, 'Some Uses of Paronomasia in Old English Scriptural Verse', *Speculum* 47, 1972, pp. 207–26.

P. Gradon, *Form and Style in Early English Literature*, London, 1971.

S. B. Greenfield, *The Interpretation of Old English Poems*, London and Boston, 1972.

S. S. Hussey, 'Langland's Reading of Alliterative Poetry', *Modern Language Review* 60, 1965, pp. 163–70.

The English Language in Medieval Literature

Index

Index

Index